TENDER
DISTANCE

A
TENDER
DISTANCE

Adventures Raising My Sons in Alaska

KAYLENE JOHNSON

Alaska Northwest Books®
Anchorage ◆ Portland

CIP information available upon request

Alaska Northwest Books®
An imprint of Graphic Arts Center Publishing Co.
P.O. Box 10306
Portland, OR 97296-0306
(503) 226-2402 * www.gacpc.com

President: Charles M. Hopkins
General Manager: Douglas A. Pfeiffer
Associate Publisher, Alaska Northwest Books: Sara Juday
Editorial Staff: Timothy W. Frew, Kathy Howard,
Jean Bond-Slaughter
Cover Design: Vicki Knapton
Interior Design: Constance Bollen, cb graphics
Production Coordinator: Susan Dupèré, Vicki Knapton

Printed in the United States of America

DEDICATION

To my sons, Erik and Mark Johnson
With wonder at the
backcountry men you've become.

Once we realize that between the closest human beings infinite distances continue to exist, a wonderful living side by side can grow up if they succeed at loving the distance between them, which makes it possible for each to see the other whole against the sky.

—RAINER MARIA RILKE

CONTENTS

Acknowledgements 9

Rendevous Peak 11

Genesis 23

Moose Meadow 37

First Salmon 51

Mount Baldy 65

Breakup 75

Porcupine Promises 87

Symphony Lake 97

Faith Falls 107

Devil's Pass 121

Kesugi Ridge 133

As Hours Will 153

Ghost Bear 163

Mount Marathon 179

Epilogue Wild Boys 195

Whatever we had missed, we possessed together the precious, the incommunicable past.

—WILLA CATHER, MY ÁNTONIA

ACKNOWLEDGEMENTS

How does one begin to express the depth of gratitude for the blessings of a life fully lived. . .to Todd, whose provision over the years made our Alaska dreams come true. Thank you. To my sons, with gratitude for the soaring memories of our years tasting the wilderness.

And for my writing friends and mentors whose encouragement and instruction nurtured this book to its completion: my writing group Marcia Wakeland, Michelle Renner-Kruse, Nanette Stevenson, Monica Devine, and Ann Dixon—for almost twenty years we've been bound by our passion for words; to Matthew Goodman, who introduced the finer aspects of craftsmanship and instilled the desire for excellence; to Dianne Aprile, who gave permission to write about the things that matter most; Luke Wallin, whose rapt attention to the songs of nature and writing taught me to listen well; to Richard Goodman for his devotion to the craft and who insisted on *le mot juste*; to Molly Peacock, whose stunning poetry and prose bolstered my courage; to Elaine Orr, who pressed for the deeper truth; and to Sena Naslund Jeter, for first choosing "Moose Hollow" for publication in the *Louisville Review*. Your belief in the good work of writing gave me the confidence to write one chapter after the next.

And finally, to my parents Joe and Gisela Cartmill and my sisters, Bettina Ferraro and Tonya Saliba, who never stopped believing. My life has been enriched by your unwavering support.

Rendezvous Peak

I did not intend to walk three hundred miles this summer. The miles just seemed to pass one after the other without my realizing how far I had hiked. In the valley where I live in Alaska, the folds and ridges of the mountains around our house are as familiar to me as the shape of my sons' ears. This summer I traced, by foot, the horizons of Eagle River and adjacent valleys. I began in late spring when tree branches held only a distant promise of green and continued through the flame of autumn. In the midst of a season in which so much had changed, I was searching for solid ground. Looking for someone I wasn't sure I would recognize.

Except for the company of an aging Labrador retriever, I hike alone—breaking my own rules for our two sons' travels in the backcountry. But the boys are off on their own adventures during this, the last summer before Erik leaves for college and life independent of our family. He will leave behind a childhood shaped by the seasons, the sculpture of the land, and the ancient pull of migration. Erik will leave during caribou season—a time after the spring calves have grown strong, but before the fall rut—when mating season will perpetuate another generation.

I have been awash in memories during these summer hikes, memories of the past eighteen years with a boy whose life has so clearly shaped my own. And my thoughts drift back to a crisp afternoon in October when a friend brought us an unexpected gift of fresh game.

Fall is both a season of brilliance and a season of death—and this day was no exception. The sun blazed through the birch trees. Leaves seemed to glow translucent from the inside, the last burn of color before the season settled into the gray and white of winter.

The entire caribou, its eyes glazed, lay in the bed of our friend's pickup. My husband Todd and I set aside what we were doing, scrubbed the countertops, and sharpened knives. Erik, who was then ten years old, watched with his younger brother, Mark, as the men hung the caribou from a tree in the backyard. The boys helped skin the animal, pulling at the hide while Todd pressed his knife blade against the membrane that fastened the fur to the caribou's body.

It takes time to put a four-hundred-pound caribou in the freezer but the work is fairly straightforward. After skinning and quartering the animal, we cut the meat into roasts, chops, and steaks. Smaller chunks were tossed into a container to be ground later for burger. The only time the job gets messy is at the site of the bullet wound. If the hunter is a sharpshooter and lucky, the shot will lodge in the animal's lungs or heart causing a quick death and minimal damage to the meat.

This animal, however, had been wounded in the hind-quarter and it was this damaged section that I was first given to process. Clotted blood and bone fragments darkened the meat. The femur was broken, the bone shattered and the marrow exposed. I fought back images of the animal trying to flee in shock and pain, its broken leg dangling. I have gotten better at this over the years—separating the concept of a living creature with the very un-living meat it provides upon its death. Our family eats fish and game year-round—an alternative to hormone-enhanced meat packaged in Styrofoam trays. Still, I cannot help but imagine the caribou alive with ears flicking one moment and then the slam of a bullet that changes everything the next.

I picked up my knife and began cutting. I had done this often enough and usually, after finding my way past those sad images, the job became an interesting lesson in anatomy. But this time, the animal's injury drew me inexplicably, deeply into the chaos of broken bone and damaged cells. The only thing separating the blood coursing through my hands from the still flesh of this animal was the fragile layer of my own skin. The wound suddenly became something more than a bloody hole in a caribou's hindquarter. It was the picture of all things broken and wounded.

Carefully I laid my knife aside and leaned against the edge of the counter. Blood throbbed in my ears like the drumbeat of time, a march toward something inevitable and true.

I took a deep breath and looked out the kitchen window. Across the valley, the mountains looked like the hunched backs of ancient mastodons, gray and weathered. Earlier in the week, snow, like powered sugar, had sprinkled their backs with "termination dust," the first snow that signifies the end of summer. The dome of blue sky seemed endless.

The back door slammed as Todd came inside carrying a roasting pan piled high with meat. Startled, I realized I was falling behind at my task. I picked up the knife and began cutting at the ragged caribou flesh, trying not to cut myself on the sharp edges of my thoughts.

In the coming weeks, as the caribou move toward their winter feeding grounds, our family will change dramatically. We will set three plates at the table instead of four. The phone will ring, at most, half as much. An eerie quiet will descend upon the household as competition ceases for the bathroom, the car, girls, and best physique. What will become of the fragile filaments that weave our family together? As one thread of our fabric pulls away I wonder how we will manage to keep from unraveling.

A first-time parent told me recently that his three-month old baby is growing cuter by the day. "I mean," he said, "he's so cute it's almost sickening."

I could tell him that this lovesickness does not diminish over the years. Children dance through our lives with wonder and joy and unholy aggravation until our spirits grow pliant and ever so tender. Children trespass and trample and try our hearts. We allow this because we love them beyond all reason. I could tell him that watching his son leave home will hurt like little else he has experienced—that the pains of childbirth never end. But I said none of these things. I just smiled and congratulated him and wished them well.

While Erik works his summer job, I find myself in his room a lot, looking at the posters on his wall, the books on his shelves, the notes he leaves lying around. The perpetual disaster area of his personal space has become very dear to me and I wrap myself in it—probably more often than is healthy. I am looking, looking, looking. Erik would, if he knew, accuse me of snooping. While I bathe in the memories of our past together, I am also searching for a glimpse of the man he is becoming. I page through the scrapbook that he plans to take to college with him. He's been working on it over the summer and it is full of pictures of friends, his brother, his dad, grandparents, girls he's known, the Alaskan landscape and his many adventures backpacking, biking, and mountaineering. I carefully place the scrapbook back in its place. In this volume of photos, amongst his friends and family, there is not one—not a single picture—of his mother.

I am looking, looking for the man he will become—without me.

Flying over caribou country for the first time in a small airplane, I was awed by the distance between horizons. A tapestry of red and gold and green undulated across a stark landscape. Marshy lakes spotted the tundra, mirroring a slate sky. It was difficult to gauge size or distance. The only trees were those along the canyons and gorges of the churning Mulchatna River. North beyond the river an odd pattern of lines began to crisscross, merge, and separate along the ground. The further north we flew, the more distinct the braided lines became. These meandering marks—like stretch marks over the belly of the earth—were the migration trails of generations of caribou. Hundreds of thousands of animals had marched across this fragile land, leaving behind paths for other generations to follow. The land that nurtured them as they traveled between their summer calving and winter feeding grounds could not completely recover from the caribou's call to ceaseless movement. The animals left behind a crosshatch of scars—not so unlike children who leave indelible trails upon our lives.

A small contingent of a larger herd grazed below us. On a hill alongside a dozen caribou stood an enormous bull. His white ruff glistened against the red-stained tundra. His thick gray-brown body reflected a summer of abundance. Bloody flaps of velvet hung from his broad antlers. As fall progressed, his antlers would become pearly and polished, weapons to brandish during the fierce and manic mating season. An emblem of strength and vigor, he was an animal near the zenith of maturity—muscular, healthy, and self-assured.

I went looking for a relic of Erik's elementary days in the woods behind his old school. His fourth-grade teacher and classmates had built an amphitheater in the forest. They designed it to fit into a pocket of landscape shaped like the cupped palm of a hand. It lay fifty yards downhill from the playground between the school and the banks of Eagle River. The class measured, then bought and cut lumber. They learned about math and ecosystems. They learned about tools and construction. They learned about teamwork. At each new development, Erik invited me to come and look at their progress. The benches were a bit lopsided, the stage was a simple clearing of the trees, but overall the amphitheater was impressive. Best of all was Erik's enthusiasm and his eagerness to share it.

So just weeks before his high school graduation, I took the dog for a walk and brought my journal to sit and write on the bench that Erik had helped to build. The upper part of the trail was nearly overgrown with alder. Further down, it disappeared into a slope of thick moss and ferns. Spring's first violets hung shyly around rocks and stumps. An underground creek trickled beneath our feet. Much to the dog's delight, the stream surfaced now and then offering fresh drinking fountains along the way. We had gone some distance before I began to wonder if I'd taken a wrong turn. I knew the amphitheater wasn't as close to the river as I had come. I backtracked carefully and at last, near the playground, the familiar form of the palm-shaped pocket of land emerged, immersed in greenery. This was clearly the place. The amphitheater, however, was gone.

I couldn't believe it. Erased were all signs of fourth-grade intrusion. I looked for the remains of benches, a wooden podium, any evidence of Erik's project. Finally I found the broken edge of a board. I turned it over, brushing moss away from the damp wood. The small remnant of memory crumbled in my hand.

Erik's departure is hardly a mortal wound. It only feels, for now, like something broken, like marrow exposed—a kind of amputation. In reality it may only be a skin flap, cut from a fingertip by the careless knife of time. I can't tell yet. For now I am studying the science of reclamation. Books about the environment, cellular biology, and healing litter the floor next to my bed. A book about caribou lies in the mix.

Erik, in the meantime, has grown a beard with surprising red streaks, possible rogue strands of DNA from his Viking ancestry. He has pierced his ear. He is broad-shouldered, healthy, and self-assured. His laugh rumbles from some deep place inside and when he is thinking, his eyes narrow and his head tilts ever so slightly. He is utterly comfortable in the wilderness, confident in wild surroundings, and fearless. Along with his scrapbook for college, he is packing his climbing gear, ice ax, and helmet. Erik is on the move, traveling migration trails of his own. He is heeding an ancient call to other lands, to feeding grounds, and places to spend the summer and winter of his life.

I took one last hike before sending Erik off to school. I could not turn around in our home without being confronted by memories and a searing sense of loss. So late in the afternoon I grabbed my pack and the dog and headed for the hills. The skies had begun to clear after a week of rain and I decided to climb Rendezvous Peak. The boys and I had attempted to climb it once when they were small, but the mountain had proven too steep for their young legs and too jagged for my maternal sensibilities. This time I decided to climb it from the other side beginning in Hiland Valley. I would climb to the top of the mountain ridge and then follow the ridge that eventually connected to the base of Rendezvous Peak.

The first part of the hike was steepest. I climbed quickly until my heart pounded and my lungs ached. I did not slow down until my breath came in ragged gasps. Plump blueberries grew on the sunny side of the slope but I ignored them. Each gulp of oxygen felt like fire in my chest. Each exhale scoured the cobwebbed corners of my mind. I wanted physical pain to muscle out all else—all thought and memory and regret. When the top of the ridge leveled out I began to run, pushing harder. The spongy tundra gave way to solid rock as I approached the base of Rendezvous Peak. The wind began to blow, which grew colder and more forceful as I neared the mountain.

I stopped, dug my jacket from my pack, zipped it closed, and pressed forward. Serrated fingers of rock jutted along either side of the trail. The dog glanced at me uneasily as the wind tore at my nylon jacket, creating a fierce flapping of fabric. Finally I crested the top. No angle on the peak offered shelter from the cold air. On clear days in winter, plumes of snow, like clouds of volcanic vapor, appear along snowy mountain crests, a testament to ferocious, unceasing winds. By now the clouds had closed in above us, blocking the sun's warm rays. Chilled, I paused only long enough to catch my breath before heading down again.

I was content now to walk instead of run. A dark cloud had given way to showers over Eagle River Valley. The wind calmed as I walked the flank of the mountain down to the ridge that led back to the trailhead. Tendrils of pale-green reindeer moss protruded from the ground looking very much like a miniature tangle of caribou antlers. On one side of the ridge lay Ship Creek Valley, a green expanse of land that dipped and rose again toward unnamed granite peaks. Hiland Valley lay on the other side of the ridge and beyond it was Eagle River Valley. My home was hidden somewhere on the distant hillside amidst trees beginning their yellow tinge toward fall. Red dogwood berries nested in the arms of white lichen.

Suddenly the sun slipped below the cloud deck. On its way to a late-evening sunset, the sun poured itself straight through the pass I was hiking. Autumn's golden light cast a hard-edged shadow against the far side of the valley. I stopped. Like a kid, I jumped and waved, wondering if my silhouette might dance along the shadow's edge. My movement was too infinitesimal to register all those miles away. I tried again, but wedged between darkness and light, my presence was indistinguishable from the mountain.

Shadows began to deepen and the air grew cool as twilight descended. A ground squirrel squeaked. The dog dashed after it with puppylike enthusiasm. Chasing after lost causes could be the end for a dog her age, but I didn't have the heart to call her back.

GENESIS

The hard dry kernels of seeds rattled in their paper packages. With hands pressed together as in prayer, I furrowed a shallow trench in the soil. The dirt was warm in Oklahoma, not cool like the northern places I was accustomed to gardening. The unfamiliar sounds of locusts buzzed and clicked in the trees. My fingers unearthed moist white grubs and I tossed them out of the cultivated patch. One seed at a time, I placed the beans two inches apart, covered them with dirt, and patted the ground before moving on to the next row.

Recent changes in my life gave me an off-balance sense that the entire universe was shifting. Trying to maintain equilibrium, I grasped the one thing that seems solid—the somewhat neglected, but familiar garden of my faith. These days I wondered a lot about God, about life's beginnings. I had an odd sense that God was not only a deity of power and might, but also a God of profound yearning. Yet what could the God who created everything possibly yearn for?

Our yard backed up against an elementary school playground. Two boys played on the other side of the chain-link fence. They used a dirt mound as a bicycle ramp, landing each jump with a clatter and cloud of dust. The boys tested how far and high they could launch their bikes. Eventually they brought a slab of old lumber and slanted it against the dirt mound. Now, they convinced each other, they'd get some real air. Somehow they reminded me of fox kits I once saw romping outside their den. Playful and daring. And like those fox kits, they took no notice of me.

"Ow!" one of the boys yelped. The board tipped like a seesaw across the mound depositing the boy and his bike with a jolt to the ground. "Oh man, that one killed my balls."

I listened, intrigued. Growing up in a family of sisters, I had never heard boys talk like this. My mother—haltingly, with color rising in her cheeks—taught us the anatomically correct terms for that odd otherness of the male gender. And my father just issued vague warnings about boys. He harbored some unspoken secret about them, some knowledge as mysterious as the inner workings of cars and the U.S. government and God—all topics over which Dad seemed to exercise great authority.

So I listened closely to the boys on bikes and realized that until now it had never occurred to me that "balls" was the right word for an eight year old. And I continued planting, wondering about the seed swelling inside my own belly.

It was 1983 when my husband Todd and I moved from Colorado to Vance Air Force Base in Enid, Oklahoma for his pilot training. Newly married, we arranged our few belongings in a tiny two-bedroom house. The walls of each room blushed a different shade of pastel. Green, plastic-backed curtains hung from the living room windows. The nap of the green shag carpeting was worn to its nubs. In those first weeks, before Todd's training began, we painted the inside of the house a scrubbed white. We painted the outside too, and talked about overturning a portion of the backyard for a garden. And we made love with the abandon of newlyweds. We had, after all, our license.

I rose early on a sunny Sunday morning in September— my twenty-first birthday—and set up the home pregnancy test. Todd slept as glass test tubes clinked in the bathroom sink. Paper crinkled as I opened the instructions. A blue ring in the bottom of the test tube meant positive; the absence of a ring meant no baby. The results would take one hour. I walked the five steps from the bathroom to the front door and collected the newspaper off the porch. A furnace blast of heat intruded into the air-conditioned house. Even in September, Oklahoma shimmered like a mirage. I sat down to read, but stared through the page. The newsprint might just as well have been hieroglyphics.

We had hardly adjusted to sleeping together, the scent of each other's bodies, the night sounds of someone else's breathing. We had known each other for four years but married life was different. So awkward. Like trying to live with an elephant in the house. Who would have guessed it would be so big? And how would we manage to squeeze parenthood into our cramped quarters? Still, some shivery place in me secretly hoped a baby was on the way. Yet would Todd, who planned with meticulous care every detail of his existence, be resentful of this dramatic change to the blueprint of his life? Just last week we argued about how to fold a bath towel properly.

Either way, whether the test results proved positive or negative, I made a promise to myself. I decided that a baby would not change us. A child would simply be an addition to our lives, a little dory pulled alongside the ship of our marriage. We'd plotted our course and had our plans. I would finish college. Todd was on his way to becoming an Air Force pilot. I couldn't have known that changing tides can set adrift even the staunchest of anchors. Or that a little star can turn out to be a planet with an orbit all its own.

Ten minutes after I sat down with the newspaper, Todd stirred, padded into the bathroom, and emerged grinning. Bare-chested and shoeless, he wore nothing but his usual sky-blue shorts to stay cool. His hazel eyes reflected some secret amusement. He said nothing, just reached for the comics and sat down across the room.

"I did the pregnancy test this morning," I said, stating the obvious. We'd talked about this for days.

His smile grew wider. "I know."

I dashed in to see what he already knew. There, at the bottom of the test tube was a distinct, indisputable ring—the color of little boy blue.

After Todd spaded the ten-by-ten-foot square, we ripped the sod out together, scraping the bottom of grass clumps to salvage topsoil. It wasn't an ambitious garden, just a small patch for fresh tomatoes, some lettuce, spinach, and green beans. The garden connected us to our Dakota upbringing. Oklahoma seemed as foreign as our new life together. Marriage, pregnancy, and pilot training created in us a homesickness for some token of familiarity. Back home, our families gardened large tracts of dark Dakota soil. We learned young how to distinguish weeds from vegetable plants. Close to harvest, my sisters and I crunched on raw peas and savored the strawberries that the robins hadn't already raided. We snuck warm tomatoes off the vine, eating them until the corners of our mouths stung from their juices.

Our little garden in Oklahoma hardly compared to the ones back home. Although we thought we could tend it jointly, the rigors of Todd's training allowed him little more time than it took for him to overturn the soil.

I missed my husband. Yet I held within my body the wonder of something we had a created together.

I threw away three raw chickens. Every one of them smelled like rotting flesh. At the third bad chicken in a week, I insisted we go back to the grocery store for a refund. Todd thrust his nose next to the yellowish, plucked skin and said, "It smells fresh to me. It's fine."

I set the corpse on the counter and bolted to the toilet just in time to lose my lunch. I puked in every public rest room in Enid, Oklahoma. I threw up on the street and in parking lots and in people's shrubs as I rode my bicycle to college classes each day. If this retching was part of some divine plan, I recanted my thoughts about God being a gentler God. Morning sickness lasted all day, every day for seven months.

Before the first fluttering of the baby's movement, even before wearing kangaroo-stretch maternity clothes, an ultrasound revealed a robust, thumb-sucking little boy. We named him Erik Thomas. Suddenly the pregnancy had a human face, a little round bottom and ten fingers and toes. Every protective instinct kicked into high gear—I crossed the street more carefully, refused to eat or drink anything except wholesome fare. I gave up coffee and chocolate and drank milk instead of diet cola. I exercised religiously.

As my belly swelled, so did my awe at this process of growing a baby. It was all happening according to an ancient, prescribed plan. And while this mysterious process had happened billions of times before, it felt no less profound to me than the creation of the world. My body housed a roommate, a human being with a will, a future, and a particular color of eyes. This roommate occasionally hiccupped in little rhythmic shudders and instinctively I reached to caress my stomach. Already Erik tested his boundaries, stretching and kicking and pushing his small fists against cramped living quarters. When I pressed, with my thumb, the hard lump of his foot protruding just below my ribcage, he pushed back.

A female fox and I made eye contact and as quickly as I saw her, she and her kits disappeared. For a moment I wondered if I'd seen them at all. At home in North Dakota, I was out for an early morning run along a gravel road several miles from town. Thirty yards beyond the road, past the ditch and a barbed-wire fence, a curve of prairie clay and dirt lay exposed to the Dakota sky. Normally, grass would have hidden the fox den, but spring was late in coming that year.

I stopped and stared at the dirt mound where just seconds earlier, fox babies had toddled around their mother in the glow of a morning sunrise. When the female saw me, she signaled her kits to take cover inside the den. Then she bounded away, her lush red tail flowing behind her like burnished silk—a decoy, trying to lure me away from her offspring. In the still of day, after crickets stopped chirping but before the incessant Dakota winds began, I watched.

Not even a minute passed before a tiny black nose emerged from the den. A kit crawled out and tentatively looked in the direction his mother had disappeared. Within seconds, a scramble of siblings followed where they proceeded to romp and wrestle and gnaw on each other. They trounced each other, tumbling down the slope of the den, then climbed back up to pounce again.

How perfectly naughty, I thought. They were testing boundaries, pushing against the limits of their living quarters. I felt a pang for the mother fox, knew I shouldn't linger here as she presumably watched me observe her offspring. How distressing that youngsters should have a will of their own. And how perfectly dangerous.

The first tender leaves broke through the ground and I kept vigil on the moisture content of the soil. The sun threatened to scorch these delicate buds. My belly was in the way now as I bent down to pick weeds.

Prayers grew more personal. While I once prayed for big things like world peace and food for the hungry, I now began to pray very specifically, "Keep this baby safe" and "Please, God, let me not throw up."

I crouched down and waddled between rows, checking the plants. At the end of each row, I rocked back on my heels and breathed deeply. Still adrift in nausea, praying at least stayed the dizzying tide of feeling completely overwhelmed. To the fatigue and morning sickness the pregnancy added fainting spells. The doctor assured me all was well, but I wondered. How could feeling this awful possibly result in a healthy child? I did not enroll for a second semester at the university. It hardly seemed important anymore.

I squeezed a handful of dirt in my fist. The garden needed water, but the slender new stalks would not withstand the force of a hose or sprinkler. I filled a watering can and listened to droplets pattering softly against thirsty soil. My hand rested on my stomach as I touched the life insistently thumping against my insides. God, I wondered, who are you?

It seemed God was a tender voice whispering into a dark womb; the kiss of life that sparked a beating heart, the sculptor of a mouth that already turned upward to smile.

Contractions began late in the afternoon, with my now enormous belly tightening like the hard skin of a basketball. Too excited to sleep, we played Monopoly most of the night with my mother who had come to usher in the birth of her first grandchild. By 5:30 a.m. the press of contractions grew uncomfortable. We moved to Lamaze level-three breathing. Just one more level and the baby would be here. So far, so good. I felt exceptionally brave. We decided to go to the hospital, ready for the final stage of labor. A spring breeze warmed my face as we climbed into the car and I thought, "It's a good day to have a baby."

After examination, the doctor said, "Looks like you're probably in labor, but just barely. We'll keep you here and break your water. That'll get things started."

I looked at Todd and all exceptional bravery evaporated.

Several hours later I clutched at bed sheets, clenching my teeth. I sent my mother away. She tensed with every contraction as she sat at my bedside, wishing as mothers do, to ease my discomfort. I could not cope with her pain as well as my own. Todd did not flinch when I could no longer lie still.

Transition is a mild word to describe the phase of labor just before the last and final pushing stage. My eyes darted from corner to corner of the room, back and forth, desperately looking for an exit. Escape from a body trying to turn itself inside out.

"Focus," Todd said. "Look at me."

My eyes refused so he put his face next to mine, willing me to look at him.

I finally looked and this epic pain, like a cleaver cutting through the bones of time, was momentarily contained. In this room. Enclosed in this moment. Bound up in two finite bodies working to free themselves from the other. A baby struggled through a dark passage toward the cold, sharp intake of his first breath. I gasped at the edge of a life forever altered by this event. Focus.

Erik came into the world squalling and peeing, covered with a white waxy substance, and smeared with blood. I had never seen anything so beautiful. The nurse deposited him on a clear tray to clean him up and I watched as Todd softly stroked his cheek. At the sound of his dad's voice, Erik stopped crying.

After carrying Erik inside my body for nine months, I expected to recognize him. But he was a stranger, an enigma. When visitors and well-wishers left, in the dark of the next night, I lay in bed, unwrapped this mysterious package, and examined my son. Tiny half-moons peeked out from beneath pink fingernails. His wrinkled feet looked as though he'd spent too much time in a bathtub. Tender ears rested against his small head like the delicate hearts of a rose. His chest rose and fell with each breath and I could see the beating of his heart against his ribs. I drank in the sight of him, ran my fingers over every part of his body.

A nurse walked in with a clipboard and I asked her about the faint bluish tint to Erik's skin. I'd heard of blue babies, children who could not inhale enough oxygen into their tiny lungs. Should I be concerned? No, she said. Your baby is just cold. Cover him back up.

My hands flew to bundle him into his sleeper and blanket and I clutched him under the covers against my body. Poor baby hadn't even whimpered with discomfort. My ignorance appalled me.

Tears stung my eyes and I prayed the most earnest prayer of my life.

"God, help me." I could not know how these words would become a mantra in the coming years.

Erik's soft cheek rested against the inside of my arm. His dark eyelashes lay like tiny fronds against the curved landscape of his face. It dawned on me that childbirth must be like death. Both journeys involve a wrenching of one life into another. An ending and a beginning, through which lies an encounter beyond all experience.

Quietly, like a seed erupting from its pod, my view of God expands beyond thunder and benevolent restraint. God is not only a father. She is a mother profoundly in love with her child.

Heat shimmered above the baked soil as I tore out weeds by the handful. Erik, two months old, napped inside. Even though it was only late July, the lettuce had long since gone to seed in the heat. Yellow flowers drooped over a pyramid of foliage. Time had double-backed on itself since the birth of my son. Erik slept only one or two hours at a time, day and night. Fatigue numbed my mind. I could not remember what day it was. Although I could have napped too, this orphaned garden demanded something from me. It was a vestige of something I began when I believed I still had the power to control some aspect of creation—at the very least, how a child would affect our lives. I tore out more weeds, but my heart was not in it. Nothing stirred in the heat. No breeze, no little boys on bikes.

Sweat trickled between my swollen breasts. Erik sometimes sputtered at the surge of milk that flooded into his mouth when he began to nurse. I could not regulate this abundance—just as I could not govern the outpouring of my fierce love for him. I brushed off my hands and went inside to check on him. I paused to watch the rhythm of his breathing.

How tenderly God must have held the soil that absorbed that holy, life-giving breath. When Adam drew in his first lungful of air in the garden, did God look him over and stroke the smooth skin of a sleeping child? Marvel at the cleft chin, the fullness of his lips?

Back outside I discovered that the green beans thrived in spite of my neglect. Their long slender fingers hung heavy beneath broad leaves. I gathered the front of my shirt into a pouch. Bean by bean, I harvested a garden of plenty.

Moose Meadows

Todd and I both made plans to run away from home and live in a hollowed out tree. We didn't know each other then, but as youngsters we had both read Jean Craighead George's *My Side of the Mountain*, an adventure novel about Sam Gribley, a boy who made a life for himself in the mountains. Sam befriended a falcon that he trained to hunt. His journey to self-sufficiency in a wild place inspired us to do the same. Todd and I grew up in the same prairie town in North Dakota. When we finally met in high school, we incredulously discovered that we had checked out the same survival books at our small public library—probably waiting impatiently for the other to return *Field Guide to Edible Wild Plants* or the lone book about falconry. Although the wide-open spaces of the Dakotas had their appeal, we both longed for mountains.

We yearned for a place we had never lived, a frontier we had never seen.

After Erik's birth, Todd finished pilot training in Oklahoma and the Air Force sent us to Little Rock, Arkansas. While the Ozarks had their own distinct beauty, we missed the imposing peaks in Colorado where we'd lived while he attended the Air Force Academy. Todd worked tirelessly to get an assignment elsewhere and I grew round with the fullness of a second pregnancy. This time the months flew by with only one foray into nausea, an embarrassing assault on the neighbor's dahlias while taking Erik for a stroll. Just as I'd wondered how our marriage would hold up with the addition of a baby, I worried how I could love another child as much I adored Erik. Yet miraculously, just as my skin somehow expanded over my growing belly, my soul stretched to accommodate this new little boy, Mark Joseph.

A tender baby, Mark was easily startled as an infant. Unless I wrapped him snuggly and held him close, his little arms flew up in terrified spasms and his hands clutched at empty air as though he were free-falling through the universe. Often, by the end of the day and overwhelmed by the sensations of a foreign world, he lapsed into crying jags and wailed until he fell into exhausted sleep.

Sometimes I knew just how he felt. Todd was often gone, this place was less familiar even than Oklahoma, and I missed my mother. Maybe she could explain why my youngest son would not be comforted, or why neither of my children slept more than a few hours at a time, or why I could not shake the feeling of homesickness even as I tried to fashion a home and family of my own.

The most reliable reprieves from melancholy were long walks with the boys. Erik rode in a stroller wearing a little white sun hat to protect his fair skin. He pointed at ducks and grebes while Mark dozed, nestled and sweating against me in a baby backpack. We walked the perimeter of a local pond, then up and down the rolling hills of the Air Force base neighborhood. Sometimes we stopped at the pond and Erik would insist on the game he and Todd played at the water's edge. I would catch a few live grasshoppers which Erik would then lob into the water. In a flash of silver, the grasshopper disappeared as a sunfish grabbed its wriggling meal. Erik never tired of this game or of feeding stale bread to the fat mallards that grew bold at the sight of a stroller and a plastic bag. This was our wilderness.

Todd finally received his assignment, one that held all the promise of our youthful desire to live in wild places. Surely Alaska would be a grand place to raise our sons—a place where prepackaged urban living had not erased the ebb and flow of a more natural life. But I learned that childhood dreams can be shaken by fears born of an unpredictable reality.

We arrived in Alaska on a sunny day in March. Erik was nearly three and Mark was just a few months past his first birthday. During the approach to Anchorage International Airport, the plane circled over the snow-covered Chugach Mountains. The waters of Cook Inlet glittered in the sunlight. Inside the airport, the *Anchorage Daily News* headlines announced that Susan Butcher had won the Iditarod—a 1,149-mile sled dog race from Anchorage to Nome. Now this was a place that would test our mettle. Here Todd could hunt and fish to his heart's content. And I could collect, like ripe succulent berries, memories of clear rivers and jagged mountains, of deep snow and the cold bite of winter air—memories that seemed to be in place long before I had experienced them. Here we could raise our children close to the land, nurtured by a natural cycle of life that would give them a clear-eyed, healthy view of the world. And here we would grow close to a Creator whose handiwork dwarfed all human invention.

The boys begged to play in the dirty snow just outside the door at the baggage claim. Todd and I grinned at each other. We knew we had finally come home.

We settled in the community of Eagle River, the name of both the river and the town perched along its banks. The Chugach Mountains rise on both sides of the valley, sentinels of the river whose headwaters trickle off Eagle glacier twenty miles upstream. In winter, the skin of the frozen river created a smooth white ribbon of ice and snow. In summer, the river grew angry, churning with glacial silt, rain, and snowmelt.

Although we treasured our wilderness backyard, we were not above using human invention to protect ourselves from Alaska's extremes. And in the process of accumulating tents, backpacks, sleeping bags, tarps, clothing–all of which in some way protected us from the elements—I reluctantly accumulated something more. Beginning on a rainy day in July, I began to collect something akin to fear.

That first summer, the boys and I made a midsummer discovery—an ample harvest of berries. The boys liked nothing more than picking raspberries and blueberries— except maybe eating them. Looking for berries held all the fun of playing hide-and-seek or hunting for Easter eggs. Every plump, juicy orb was a prize.

Erik especially savored the taste of blueberries, plucking them off the bush and popping them into his mouth. He announced one day that he would be a blueberry farmer when he grew up. I believed him. Already, his eyes were the color of blueberries, his rosy face embraced by wheat-colored hair. His gentle nature made it easy for me to imagine him bent over fields of shrubs, nurturing them to produce his favorite food. It would likely be an unprofitable enterprise, though. Few berries actually found their way into his bucket. After he picked berries for awhile, he sidled up to my pail and asked, "Do you need *all* of those to make jam?"

Mark, whose arrival followed Erik's birth by only eighteen months, refused his status as younger sibling. Having outgrown his infant insecurities, he fearlessly attempted every skill his brother already possessed. At five months he crawled; at nine he walked. With his determined athleticism, his soft baby features quickly gave way to the more angular shape of a little boy. His enormous eyes, a darker blue than Erik's, reflected every passing mood, either sparkling with jubilation or glowering with indignation. When he slept, with intense eyes closed, Mark appeared wholly at peace—a tender contrast to his smoldering personality.

Mark picked berries too, but after collecting what he considered a fair amount (half a cup or so) and eating another pint, he flicked berries at his brother. In the echo of Mark's belly laughs, Erik happily reciprocated. Not thrilled about the wasted berries, I suggested that if they must throw things, at least chuck crow berries—something we wouldn't use to make jam.

On this particular rainy day, we wandered into an a patch of raspberries and settled into picking. I breathed deeply the clean scent of rain. The boys squatted under a canopy of foliage where raspberries grew thick under an overhang of alders and scrub willow. Steeped in shrubbery, the only opening in this mass of greenery lay several feet behind us. The drizzling rain muffled our voices, pattering softly on the hoods of our jackets.

I did not hear, until the sound was very close, the approaching crash of a large animal moving through the brush. My first thought was a bear. We were, after all, in bear territory and very possibly trespassing in some bruin's favorite berry patch. Instinctively, I grabbed the boys by the nape of their raincoats and pulled them toward me.

"Go on! Get out of here!" It surprised me that my voice sounded so loud and fierce with alarm clutching at my throat.

In two steps I rose out of the brush to face whatever thundered toward us. As my head came up into the clearing, I nearly bumped into the elongated nose of a mother moose, her spring calf trotting at her side. She stopped abruptly and snorted. A grown moose can stand six feet at the shoulder, and this mom was no exception. We eyed each other for an instant. The brown fur on her neck and shoulders bristled. Her ears pressed against her head as she considered a charge.

"Move it! Get out of here!" I shouted, waving my arms. Startled, she lept away and crashed back into the brush.

Still in my grip, the boys were too low to the ground, and the brush was too thick for them to see. "What was that, Mom?" Erik asked, blueberry eyes wide with surprise.

"It sounded very big," Mark said, his hands clasped together, his shoulders rounded.

The most dangerous animals in the world are females protecting their young. A mother moose with a calf is potentially as dangerous as a bear. I suddenly realized that in a confrontation between mothers of the wilderness and a mother of suburbia, I possessed absolutely nothing with which to defend my own babies. I sank down on wobbly knees and tried not to sound panicked.

"It was a mama moose and her calf," I said. "She's gone now. I think we scared her pretty good."

"I think she scared *us*," Mark said, always quick to the truth of the matter.

We went through the motions of berry picking a little longer with the boys hanging close. I carried on without a fuss. I didn't want the boys to develop any apprehensions about the outdoors. Yet, I could not rid myself of the coppery taste of fear in my own mouth.

Relieved to get back into the car, I buckled the boys into their car seats. They struck up a conversation with each other, a cheerful banter in the background of my thoughts. As wipers squeaked against the windshield, I decided that I could not, in good conscience, take my children into wild areas without some way to protect them. Wild mothers had hooves or claws or teeth to defend their young. I needed something to even the odds. I needed a gun.

My reluctance to handle guns has always baffled my hunter husband. To Todd, a hunting rifle is an extension of his body, a natural outgrowth of his upbringing. As a five-year-old, he hunted the Dakota Badlands next to his father. At age twelve he shot a grouse of his own, bringing dinner to the table with pride. At fourteen he bagged his first deer. The venison offered a month of meals and deep satisfaction that he had provided something of great value to the family.

My dad hunted too and, as a kid, I sometimes accompanied him. But I developed no love for the sport. It was too raw. Even as a girl, the struggle between life and death seemed epic; I always felt the weight of something profound and sad each time we successfully came home from the field.

When my dad showed me how to shoot a gun, his first priority was to teach safe handling. I was about eleven years old when dad drove us to a hilly area outside of town. Cottonwood leaves rustled in the ever-present Dakota breeze. We climbed out of the pickup and set up a few empty soda cans thirty yards away. After we had our targets in place, he picked up the .22 and told me to look into the long, dark barrel of the rifle. From earlier hunting trips with him, I knew enough never to place myself in the line of fire. The idea of putting my face at the shooting end of a cold rifle—even an unloaded one—stiffened me with fear. Dad insisted. Quickly I looked, and backed away.

"What do you see?" he asked.

"Mmm. Nothing," I answered.

"Look again," he said. "Look hard."

I took a second, longer look.

"What do you see?" he persisted. I stood still, not understanding what he was getting at.

Dad's eyes grew hard and bore straight through me.

"What you see here," he said, "is *death*."

Yes, yes I saw it now. Not just the death of animals, but my own life collapsing in on itself. I felt a dark vacuum stealing my breath away and I wanted to bound away, far, far away like a panicked deer.

In the time between learning to shoot a gun and now, I left hunting endeavors to the guys—my dad, my husband, his dad, and brothers-in-law. This rite of fall was their connection to the outdoors, a glad and natural harvest. To me it reflected the dark but certain reality that plants and animals die in order for me and my family to live. And while I conceded the natural cycles of life, I found other things to do, other connections to life and to the land. After all I had two little boys to care for and a flower garden. Our yellow flop-eared puppy chewed on the boys' shoes and the rabbit twitched her nose in the hutch outside. Entwined in all this growing, the world seemed fertile and benign.

But now, in a wooded glade, a mother moose and I squared off in response to an immediate threat to our offspring. She clearly had the advantage. My will hardly matched her weapons of size and strength. Although the grim possibilities in our encounters with nature chilled me, I refused to forgo these excursions. I was left with the only option I knew.

My .41 caliber pistol weighs about three pounds, the weight of a solid dictionary.

The six hollow-point bullets that fit in the chamber weigh a little less than one ounce each. It is a double-action revolver—when I squeezed the trigger several things happen simultaneously. The cylinder rotates, putting a bullet in line with the firing pin. Pulling the trigger both cocks and releases a thumb-shaped device called the hammer. When the hammer hits the firing pin, it slams against a small circular primer on the flat end of the bullet. The spark caused by this impact ignites the gunpowder inside the brass cartridge, sending the bullet out the chamber at a velocity of 1,275 feet per second. Hollow-point bullets expand on impact, inflicting more tissue damage than other types of bullets.

And so I placed faith for my sons' safety in a cold metal man-made device. The gun became my answer to a bear's six-inch claws, four-inch incisors, and jaws big enough to enclose a human head. To a moose's hooves, sharp and broad as a child's face.

A pistol emptied into a moose at close range will kill the animal. When it comes to bears, however, old-timers known as "sourdoughs" will tell you that if you manage to draw your gun soon enough and if, with shaking hands, you can aim at a moving target, pumping six rounds of a .41 caliber bullet into a charging grizzly will only piss him off. These folks maintain that only a shotgun at close range and loaded with lead slugs—like a handheld cannon—will stop a bear.

Todd, who once spent a long night with bears trying to break into his cabin, scoffs at anyone who refuses to take a gun into the backcountry. He maintains that this approach is not only naive, but irresponsible. Still, I would rather believe in a natural world in which, if I intend no harm, no harm will come, where other creatures and I respect each other's space without animosity. Mostly this is true.

What is also true is that with all the life-affirming possibilities of wilderness expeditions comes the possibility for disaster. Erik and Mark happily placed complete confidence in this weapon I now carried with us. They never failed to ask whether I had it along. Their apprehension quickly dissipated with my assurance that yes, the gun was in my pack. The weight of my own fear was not so easily assuaged, however. Carrying a gun seemed an entirely false faith. All it really provided was the knowledge that should anything happen, I could at least say I tried.

That was part of the trouble. The moment I opened my mind to the possibility of one disaster, others began to loom their sinister heads. So while the kids romped on the spongy tundra, climbed trees, or pelted each other with berries, I cast wary glances over my shoulder.

I suppose someday I will hike the backcountry without my sons. I imagine the cow moose as she feeds on a stand of willows, bordering a lush undergrowth of currant bushes. The sweet scent of rain hangs in the air. The moose takes note of my presence and returns to stripping newly washed leaves from the willow branches. The deadly force with which I was willing to protect my young will dissipate once again into respectful awareness. Both our offspring have found other glades in which to play. And this time, I will leave the gun at home.

First Salmon

Even before the electrical impulse, before the spark of life created movement—before a flick of tail or fin—her eyes stared beyond the membrane of her embryonic cocoon. She saw the graveled texture of her redd, a cradle created by her mother in the bed of a freshwater stream. She saw gradations of light as the long days of summer moved toward winter. She saw shadows: a dark moose's hoof as it narrowly missed her bed; the swipe of a bear's paw; the silhouette of eagles' wings passing overhead. And she saw the mottled shapes of adult salmon moving laboriously through cold water. Birth and death happened simultaneously here in the hushed eddy of this quiet stream. But she could not know this, as knowing goes, the primordial cycle of life and death. She could only see with eyes around whose forms a body slowly grew.

In late winter, the stream's pristine waters maintained a steady temperature under a thin slice of ice that closed the river to predators and other hazards. On top of the ice lay three feet of snow. Underneath, a translucent head as well as a slender body and tail emerged from the salmon's bright orange egg sac. She could move now, but only in flickers, as she and her alevin siblings grew crowded under their protective gravel sheath. Still the most prominent features of her body were golden eyes, huge and unblinking, which absorbed the very essence of this place. Somehow she would remember it all, assimilate every detail about these waters, the scent of the seasons, the colors of rock and snow and sky. Although her body fed on the ever-shrinking yolk, something beyond the fullness of these nurtured days of growth began to stir in her cells. Something akin to longing.

The gray of winter dissolved into the brilliant sparkle of spring as lengthening daylight melted the snow and ice. In a desperate press against the confines of her watery womb, the salmon—barely the length of a human fingertip—dislodged first one and then another pebble. The current, made stronger by snowmelt and rain, gently pried the rest of the redd apart. Suddenly she found herself swept up and away by rushing water. Instinctively, she shuddered and flexed and then swam. Yet her strength was nothing against the power of water and she tumbled downstream until the current deposited her into a shallow back eddy several yards from where she had hatched. Her tiny gills heaved with the free-falling sensation of a universe breaking open, beckoning. She was, for the first time, hungry.

Our four-year-old son, Erik, suffered one frustration after the other, trying to catch the bountiful and yet elusive salmon. Our family had watched from the viewing deck of Ship Creek as salmon leapt Herculean heights against the current to clear a waterfall that blocked their upstream passage. Again and again, the salmon threw themselves against the white water, and inwardly I cheered each time one of them cleared the falls. Their journey home seemed both noble and incomprehensibly difficult. They had traveled far into a wide ocean world. And yet here they were, willing to dash themselves against raging falls to return to the small stream or eddy where they first hatched. I remembered how Alaska had felt like home from the very first moments our family arrived here a few short years earlier. And I wondered to what extent migration was a part of my own life. While I considered the movement of body and soul, Erik thought of only one thing: he wanted to catch a fish.

Ship Creek was closed to fishing, so we decided to try our luck at one of the most popular fishing streams in Alaska. Sockeye salmon choked the stream where fishermen were known to stand shoulder to shoulder in a stance known as "combat fishing." It was our first try. The season opened at noon, and knowing how popular the fishing hole was, we came early and parked ourselves along a grassy curve in the river. Slowly, more fishermen began to filter in, and as the clock's hands moved toward noon, Erik positioned himself on a tuft of shoreline protruding from the bank. Just moments before the appointed time, a man in waders stepped in front of Erik, making it impossible for him to cast his fly into the water. Another man joined the first, and soon a wall of fishermen blocked any shore-side access to the river.

I was incensed. "How rude," I said. "Can't you give a little boy room to cast?" With downcast eyes, the fishermen ignored us.

While I fumed over Erik's dilemma, the noon opening began. The river became a boil of salmon as fish fought at the end of dozens of lines that had dropped simultaneously. Fishermen called, "Fish on," a warning for neighboring anglers to pull their lines from the water until the salmon could be landed.

After two hours of waiting with anticipation, and now standing three feet behind the chaotic action, Erik started to beg. Couldn't we please carry him, just hold him as we stood in the water with our own waders while he cast his line?

Meanwhile, his two-year-old brother Mark leaned over the bank's edge, grabbing for smolt that darted through icy waters. As we tried to comfort Erik and come up with a new plan, Mark overreached and, with a splash, toppled into the river.

My husband Todd retrieving our wailing toddler by the scruff of his life jacket said, "This just isn't going to work."

I agreed. "Let's go."

Erik buried his face in my shoulder and wept.

She spent her summer days foraging, picking at plankton and any-thing else that might nourish her ravenous growth. Between the hours and days of continuous browsing came spasms of panic as predators feasted on the fry. Eagles and seagulls regularly scooped fingerlings into their craws. Ducks and a family of young otters fed on the tender fish. Somehow, with skittish luck, she managed to flash past probing beaks and snapping teeth.

Later in the summer, piscine freighters moved into the stream, and she knew to stay out of the way as adult salmon began their spawning rituals. Females riffled their tails through the gravel, creating nests for their young. Males fought each other for the opportunity to lay milt upon the eggs. The adults' stately movements were tinged with deep fatigue. Many of the older fish were already fading in color as the life force leeched from their bodies. After spawning, they deteriorated even further. Chunks of graying flesh hung from their washed-out forms.

But the smolt grew bolder. Something about the scent of older fish drew her closer, something familiar yet strange. A spawned-out salmon lay on its side. Its tail waved feebly and occasionally—just enough to keep it from turning completely belly up. She approached the dying fish and on impulse nuzzled a gash in its back. Obeying a mysterious and ancient dictum, she then opened her mouth and began to feast.

Back at our Russian River camp, I changed Mark into dry clothes and wiped Erik's red-rimmed eyes and runny nose.

Todd broke down the fishing rods while I made sandwiches at the picnic table.

I could not recall when I had been so angry with strangers. Wasn't fishing a way to connect with earth's bounty, an opportunity to reflect on the natural rhythms of life? Wasn't catching that very first fish a rite of passage, an initiation they too had enjoyed as children? Yet these people behaved as though they might not survive the coming winter if they did not haul in a truckload of salmon. Judging by the fish churning this river, weren't there enough for everyone?

I later learned that while 150 million wild salmon return each year to Alaskan waters, the Russian River is one of only a handful of in-state salmon streams accessible without boat or small aircraft. So fishermen without these expensive accoutrements flock to it like hungry gulls.

As I cut the boys' sandwiches into halves, a tall white-haired man approached, wondering if we might loan him a fingernail clipper.

"Sure," Todd said, reaching into his pocket.

"Would you mind clipping the line from this fly?" he said.

He turned his head to show us a 1½-inch fishhook imbedded in the cartilage of his ear. A string of fishing line hung from the hook's eyelet.

"That line—it's bothering me something awful," he said.

Horrified, Todd snipped the line and asked if he needed a ride to the emergency room.

This man had just been at the Russian River fishing shoulder-to-elbow with others. A woman next to him cast her line, accidentally hooking him in the ear. Rather than offer an apology, she had clipped the line, tied on another fly and continued to fish.

"I think I've had about enough fishing in this place," he said.

We nodded. This wasn't fishing. This was madness.

After growing sleek and silvery, something in her cells told her it was time to leave this place. So she, along with what remained of her siblings, slipped downstream toward a vastness they could not comprehend, toward saline waters that had called and sheltered generations of their forebearers. Yet she and the others did not travel headlong toward the ocean. Instead, they allowed the current to push them tail first downstream. As the water swept her toward her future, she looked with lidless eyes at the place of departure. And she remembered.

In the ocean, she joined other salmon her age and size. Here, the dangers were just as numerous as in the stream of her birth. But she moved freely now, not bound by narrow banks. She traveled in a school that flashed its shiny flank like one enormous organism. Whales, sharks, seals, dolphins, and sea lions preyed on it, taking their fill but still leaving bountiful numbers for the next predator. In these waters she grew strong and muscular. Her flesh deepened to a rich shade of red as her body readied itself for a long sojourn. Her scales shimmered like a polished coat of armor. The ocean's munificence fortified her, and she grew larger than her freshwater home would have allowed. As one and then another year passed, she learned the sea's dangers. She might have been content to stay put indefinitely, except that, as seasons turned, the memory of freshwater began to pull at her. Egg follicles formed inside of her and with them, desire. Earth and water directed her; the low voltage of the planet's magnetic aura and the moon's sway over the tides stirred her. Finally, as she and her kin traveled closer to shore, she caught a scent that propelled her forward: the scent of home.

Later that the summer, we heard about a small, salmon-rich slough off the Knik River. Retreating tides lowered the water level, creating elongated pools along the mouth of the river. Salmon swam circles in these watery pens, locked in by sand and gravel until the next tide reopened the river's corridors. It seemed like a perfect place for a little boy to catch a fish.

We arrived late in the day, at low tide, determined to stay as long as Erik wanted to. The summer sun accommodated our plans. At that time of year, after a rosy midnight sunset, the pale glow would travel just below the horizon across the northern sky until it popped up again as a fiery ball over the eastern mountains.

Erik cast his pixie into the pool. The spoon lure sparkled through clear water as he slowly reeled it back to shore. He cast over and over, with the ease of someone who had been born to fish. He fished with resolve, trying different pixies, casting from different positions around the pool. But no matter what he tried, the salmon were indifferent to his hook. Todd helped him to change lures and untangled the occasional nest of fishing line in the reel.

Mark had long since grown bored, so he and I scouted the riverbed for other treasures—rocks, seaweed, and muddy puddles to jump in. Even I was growing restless while Erik and Todd exhausted all venues of catching salmon.

As the evening grew cooler, I marveled at Erik's determination. His intensity seemed to reflect the migration of salmon itself. I suspected that somehow, in some ancient but now latent genetic code, humans had been wired to harvest rivers. Erik, at least, seemed to have tapped into some primal and insistent aspect of his nature.

"Mom," he called. "Could you come here?"

"Sure," I said.

"Here," he said, pointing at the muddy ground. "Right here."

I kneeled next to him wondering what he had in mind. Still casting what was now a pink pixie, he sidled up to me and leaned heavily against my shoulder.

"What do you need, Erik?" I asked.

Erik sighed deeply. "I need you to hold me up," he said.

Too tired even to stand, he refused to give up his quest for salmon. Only with firm and solemn promises that we would soon return did we convince him that, perhaps, it was time to go home.

In estuary waters her desire grew pressing. She stopped feeding. Drawing on memory ingrained in her DNA, she knew she had been here before. And she knew where she was headed. Muscling upstream against the current, water washed through her gills in a rush of oxygen and urgency. All she had seen on her backsliding journey to the ocean now rematerialized. She charged into the sprinting water, leapt over rocks, dove under fallen trees. As eggs swelled in her body, her urgency became a sort of rage, an aggression that dared the very stars to keep her from reaching her destination.

As she expended stored supplies of fat, as hormones and enzymes surged through her blood, her body transformed. Her flesh paled while her scales turned the color of fireweed in fall, an unrelenting flame. Her head changed from a smooth, stretched-out U to an angry and angular V. She appeared formidable, yet not nearly as fierce-looking as her male cohorts, which sprouted jagged teeth along hooked jaw lines. Like her, they drove forward but not before shimmying against her, testing to see if the time for courtship had arrived. Although the home scent grew stronger, she was not content in any waters except those lodged in her memory since the moment of conception.

Finally—battered and bruised by miles of upstream struggle—she arrived. With great deliberation, she dug her redd, accepted a mate, and then released eggs into the gravel bed. The last of the fury that had propelled her was spent. The kinder waters of the eddy soothed her. Her battle was over and she could rest.

The summer after Erik failed to catch his first salmon we tried again, this time along the banks of the Little Susitna River. We camped on an island, cradled by stream channels, at a place where we could cast our lines with minimal interference from rapacious fishermen. Erik flung his lures as we set up our tent. Mark climbed an alder tree, trying to entice his brother to join in the fun. Erik ignored him.

I watched my son's intent and focus, his movements, fluid as water. A year had passed since his last attempt to catch a salmon, and both boys now were an inch taller. Eventually, we convinced Erik to eat and come to bed. We had the whole weekend to fish. In the middle of the night, we woke to the patter of rain on the tent. Slowly, it grew louder and more insistent, until sheets of rain pelted the flapping nylon. By 2 a.m. water began to seep through the seams of the floor. By 3 a.m. our sleeping bags lay in cold, muddy puddles. We worried more about access back to shore than we did about the dripping tent. To get to the island, we had walked in hip waders, carrying the boys piggyback across a twenty-foot channel. As more rain fell the water rose, and we feared we might need a boat to get off the island.

The next morning, with rain still lashing the water and the river rising, we packed up and began hauling our gear back to the mainland and up the mile-long trail to the car. This time, we nearly swamped our waders. Perched on our backs, the kids had to lift their feet to keep their boots dry.

Erik's disappointment was cavernous. Hadn't we promised he could fish the next morning? He hadn't caught a single salmon. Not last summer. Not this summer. Not one.

After crossing, Erik pleaded to fish from shore while we carried our gear to the car. A middle-aged couple that stood several yards downstream from where we had crossed assured us they would keep an eye on Erik if he wanted to fish for a while. We agreed and strapped a life vest to his slender frame. Perhaps twenty minutes of casting would lessen his frustration at leaving the salmon behind.

The current now was slow-moving clear mountain water. From behind rocks, smolt appeared. Tentative at first, they became more intrepid at her sluggishness. Her body had grown so heavy, almost too cumbersome to move. All that remained of her will had shriveled into the slow, occasional swish of her tail. Eventually even that grew tiresome, and she lay limp, sideways, suspended in the shallows. The only life left glimmered from

her eyes, the same eyes that had first registered light and shadow
here. Motionless, she watched. As still as she had been in the
beginning, she absorbed the swirling, took in the colors of rock
and sky—and watched unblinking as a new generation fed on
her flesh.

The cry of a seagull pierced the evening air. And down-
stream, a little boy fished, hoping that maybe this time he'd
finally catch one.

Returning from our second load to the car with Mark in tow,
Erik met us with wide eyes and a breathless smile.

"I got one!" he said.

"No!" I answered.

"Yup. It's right there, in the grass."

Todd and I looked at each other and then at the couple
whose grins reflected Erik's joyful surprise. Sure enough—in
the tall green grass there lay a large chum salmon.

"Your boy did a great job," the man from downstream
said. "He kept the rod tip up and held the line tight until I
could get to it with my net. It's the only fish I've seen caught
all day."

I couldn't believe I'd missed it, missed the sight of
Erik's face as the force of twelve pounds detonated against
his line. How his young arms must have pumped the rod and
flown at the reel with the salmon's lurching and diving. I felt
my throat constrict. My sons had become the port at which

I'd anchored my deepest sense of purpose. Was it possible that, already, Erik was embarking on a migration of his own? That this was just the beginning of a long and tender leave-taking?

Erik slid his fingers under the salmon's blood-red gills and hefted it up for us to see. Held chest-high, the size of the salmon nearly eclipsed his five-year-old body. The sleek fish glistened the color of chrome. Bands of green and purple striped its sides. Erik could only hold it up for a few seconds before dropping it back onto the damp grass.

With arching gestures, my son described his battle with the salmon, how it had almost pulled him into the river, and how it had struggled first up- and then downstream before he managed to reel it in. Squatting next to his prize, he slowly smoothed his hand across the cool wet scales. Quietly, with a hint of reverence, he said, "This is a very fine fish."

Mount Baldy

The boys and I crept one small step at a time toward the peak's summit. Our day had not begun as a quest, just an afternoon outing to gather blueberries. But Mount McKinley rose on the horizon 120 miles away, inspiring me to try and trek to the top of our local berg. The distance to the top was about a mile with an elevation gain of 1,400 feet. Yet, for a three- and five-year-old, it might just as well have been the tallest mountain on the continent.

The rounded peak sparked the interest of Erik and Mark who could view Mount Baldy from nearly every direction in our little town. The mountain marks the outermost peak of a ridge that reaches into the Meadow Creek and Eagle River valleys. In winter, Baldy shimmers in the sunshine, smooth and white as a scoop of ice cream. When April and May's perpetual daylight awakens spring, we watch a playful green creep up the hillside. In fall, colors descend from the top as red, yellow, and orange foliage spread downward like slow-moving flames. When fall reaches the timberline, the birch and alder turn golden, lighting up the base of the mountain with a lopsided crown of color. And in summer, well in summer, we picked berries.

From time to time throughout our season of light, Erik asked, "Are the berries ripe yet?" He snacked all winter on store-bought frozen blueberries. The idea of eating them ripe off the bush, in unlimited quantities, filled his eyes—the very color of blueberries—with delight.

"They'll be ready in a few more weeks," I said. "In August. Then we can pick berries."

It was like waiting for Christmas.

August finally arrived and we packed our berry buckets, our water bottles and snacks, and headed to the mountain. The weight of the gun in my pack reminded me that we were hiking in the wilderness. We sang "Baby Beluga," making noise to avoid a wildlife encounter. Alder and willow cloaked the first few hundred yards of the trail and we dodged branches as we made our way toward the timberline.

Erik happily led the way to what he hoped would be the best blueberry patch ever. Mark stomped close behind, his dinosaur backpack hugging his small frame. Inside he carried his beloved stick-knife, a worn piece of wood that fit neatly in the palm of his hand.

"If I get lost, I can hunt for food," he said, brandishing the stick like a dagger. His three-year-old legs pumped overtime to keep up with his older brother.

As we emerged from the trees into low alpine tundra, a partial view of Eagle River and the Knik Arm of the Cook Inlet lay before us. On the far horizon, the white peak of Mount McKinley pierced an azure sky. Locals call it Denali, an Athabascan word meaning "The High One."

We stopped to catch our breath and sip from our water bottles.

"Look guys," I said. "There's Denali."

"Is it as tall as Baldy?" Erik wondered.

"Way taller," I explained. "It's the tallest mountain in North America."

It was the summer after Vern Tejas made the first successful solo winter ascent of Mount McKinley. Just a few months earlier, I had found myself paying special attention to newspaper and radio reports tracking his whereabouts on the mountain. For days Alaskans waited and wondered. Did his delay in returning to base camp mean he was dead? Other mountaineers had already died attempting this nearly impossible quest.

Something about Tejas's exploits both thrilled and appalled me. Why would anyone attempt such a thing? What was the point of being deathly cold for weeks on end?

Of battling hurricane-like winds and windchills of minus 90 degrees? Of being swallowed up by a crevasse? It all seemed so foolish. Tejas's boasted no particular reason for climbing the peak except that it hadn't been done solo before during the winter. At age thirty-five, with fifteen years of mountaineering experience in Alaska, he once said, "Mountaineering isn't logical. It doesn't make sense. It doesn't *prove* a thing, and it doesn't do a thing."

And yet . . .

The boys and I continued up the hillside until Erik discovered berries. Like a bear cub, he plopped down in the middle of the patch and helped himself, scooping handfuls into his mouth. A light breeze played with his blonde hair, blowing wisps around his intent face. Before long a purple stain of blueberries rimmed his mouth. Mark dug into my bag of trail mix, crunched on M&Ms, and then gleefully threw berries at his brother.

Vern Tejas climbed McKinley wearing a sixteen-foot aluminum ladder around his waist. The ladder served as a safety device to keep him from tumbling into a crevasse. If snow gave way across a chasm of ice and snow, the ladder would keep him suspended at ground level and provide a bridge to cross. The ladder also served as a tow bar for a sled, and a roof for the snow caves he built at each campsite.

I thought about how different my life was from this mountain adventurer. Eight years my senior, he had already made a dozen summer trips to the summit of McKinley. To get in shape for his winter McKinley climb, Tejas scaled Mount Aconcagua in Argentina three times in a row: the first time he guided a group; the second time he packed up a bicycle and rode it down; and the third time he launched himself off the mountain to parasail back to base camp. Just for fun.

I, on the other hand, had my hands full trying to parent two young boys, often single-handedly with a husband who frequently traveled. My aspirations to climb never involved anything technical. I just wanted to make some backpacking excursions. But so far, the pinnacle of our adventures involved only short hikes and afternoon outings for berry picking.

It felt strange to have already surrendered the call of adventure to the demands of domesticity. It's not that I would have traded anyone's life for my own. But Tejas's expedition had me wondering. How would I handle the incessant roar of wind known to drive climbers mad? How would I manage the relentless solitude that comes from being bunkered in a snow cave, waiting days for a storm to abate?

"Hey guys, what do you say we try to make the summit of Baldy?" I asked.

Erik's blueberry patch was nearly picked over. Mark, who

had spilled his bucket, sidled up to mine and began to help himself.

"Are there blueberries up there?" Erik asked.

"Oh, I imagine there are lots," I said, not at all sure. But a surge of ambition drew me toward the mountain's top, a desire that felt daring, even a little reckless.

"I don't want any more berries," Mark said. "I'm stuffed."

"If we go to the top, we'll be like the mountain climbers on Denali," I said. "You're good mountaineers. Look how far we've already come." Maybe some encouragement would entice the boys farther along the trail.

Mark peered across the horizon. "I think we're as high as Denali."

"Not quite," I said.

The boys agreed to climb to the top. As we plodded one small step at a time, I explained how mountaineers often place their country's flag at the summit, especially the first time anyone makes it that far or that high.

When Tejas, battered by storms and days behind schedule, finally made it to the top of Denali, he placed a Japanese flag at the summit to honor Naomi Uemura, the first person ever to climb McKinley alone in the winter. A world-famous mountaineer, Uemura last spoke with a pilot circling overhead, telling the pilot he had made it to the top. Then, during his descent of the mountain, he disappeared. His body was never found. Getting to the top of the mountain is only half the trip.

When Erik and Mark's energy waned, we stopped for a drink and a handful of trail mix. We were high enough now to see most of Eagle River and I pointed out familiar landmarks like the post office and the blue metal roof of the grocery store.

As we neared the upper third of Baldy, Erik abandoned thoughts of more berries. Berry bushes grew sparse as the landscape gave way to rockier terrain. Besides, he had caught the spirit of wanting to make it to the top. Mark, on the other hand, trudged on with mounting weariness. He required three steps for every one of mine. He climbed with hands and feet over the rocks that I could easily step over. I carried him piggyback for a while, but as the slope grew steeper, I knew it was safer to let him manage on his own. I followed him closely, encouraging him and giving him a boost from behind when he needed it.

Erik grew tired of waiting for us and disappeared over the next mound of rock.

"Erik!" I called. "Wait up. Don't go any farther."

A moment later he peered back over the ridge. "C'mon Mark," he says. "I can almost see the top."

Vern Tejas grew impatient with the storms that continually delayed his climb. In the hours and days that he was holed up in his snow shelters, he played his harmonica. Cleaned his fingernails. Did push-ups. Tried to sleep. He had already burned all the storm days he'd planned for the entire trip. After eight days in one shelter, when the winds had diminished slightly, Tejas decided to move. He left the shelter in a complete whiteout. At 12,500 feet, he maneuvered his way past several crevasses by throwing a four-foot wand like a spear ahead of him. Normally used as a route marker, the wand would land either higher, or lower, or disappear altogether.

"I want to go home," Mark said. A storm gathered on his brow, that look he had when he'd made up his mind about something and no amount of coaxing would change it.

The hike had begun to feel like a quest. If Vern Tejas could make it to the summit of McKinley in the dead of winter, surely my sons and I could climb Baldy on a sunny summer afternoon.

"You can do this, Mark," I said firmly.

The trail dissipated into a boulder-strewn hillside, a sure sign we were within a few hundred yards of the top. I knelt to let Mark use my knee as a step when suddenly his foot slipped and he fell forward against the mountain, striking his head on the rocky ground.

Mark began to wail, and Erik made his way down to check on his brother. Mark clutched his arm around my neck and dampened my shirt with his tears. Suddenly I knew with a sinking and clear conviction that I had asked too much. Pushed too hard. A closer look revealed a scrape on Mark's head. His elbow was bloody.

I looked at the boys and said. "It's time to go home."

Erik was incredulous. "But we haven't made it to the top yet."

"Close enough," I said. "We'll try again another day."

"Can I go ahead and meet you back here? It won't take long."

"No." What appeared to be the top of the mountain might only be a false summit. Besides, the first rule of mountaineering is to know your limits.

Now Erik burst into tears. He had sacrificed an hour of berry picking to make the summit and now we were turning back? Two sobbing children followed as I descended Baldy, defeated.

Tejas returned to Anchorage to a hero's welcome. It took him a grueling month to climb McKinley. To some his conquest seemed insane. To others it was inspirational. A testament of the human spirit to press against all physical and mental limits, against the boundaries even of reason. Whatever people's opinions, the entire community breathed a collective sigh of relief when he made it safely off the mountain.

Hiking down Baldy taxed us nearly as much as going up. Instead of hiking behind Erik and Mark, I now took the lead, picking our way carefully down the steep hill. My conscience grew ever more bruised as a goose-egg-sized bump began to swell under the scrape on Mark's forehead. Erik swung his arms in a discouraged huff. Real mountain men don't give up. Besides, we barely had enough blueberries to cook a batch of jam.

"We'll be back," I said. "I promise."

It was a year before we attempted to climb Baldy again. When we did, Erik climbed with a vengeance. Not even ripening blueberries kept him from the summit this time. Mark, now a four-year-old, needed a few breaks but handily reached the top. Perched, with legs dangling over the rocks that marked the mountain's peak, we dug snacks out of our backpacks. Below us the winding path of Eagle River spread into a braided delta as it meandered its way to the Inlet. The ocean glittered in the sunlight. To the north, the Alaska Range sat on the shelf of the horizon, an invitation to white dreams against a deep blue sky. The entire universe lay at our feet.

Breakup

A season called "breakup" precedes Alaska's spring, bringing days of mud and bluster. The silence of winter gives way to the enchanted trickle of melting snow. Black ravens head for the hills as white seagulls move inland. Buds swell on the trees, yet it will be another month before they burst from their pods. Windows fly open, bicycles come out of storage, and tulips boldly begin sprouting in south facing gardens. It is hard to come indoors, difficult to sleep when tendrils of sunlight now reach late into the night.

On this warm day in April 1993 the streets and bicycle trails were dry in our neighborhood. Erik, who was nearly ten years old, and Mark who had just turned eight, along with their friend Jake, nine, decided to play at a tiny creek that bubbled from an underground spring near the bike trails. Erik and Jake had just eaten lunch and fidgeted at the door, eager to get outside into the warm sunshine. Mark—always the last one to finish—sat at the table eating a grapefruit. Jake borrowed a pair of Mark's rubber boots and pulled them on, his socks still flopping off the ends of his toes.

"Hurry up, or we'll leave without you," Erik warned.

"No you won't," Mark replied confidently.

"Yes we will," Jake said.

"Ha!" Mark said. "Mom won't let you."

"Don't be so sure," I said. "Stop talking and finish your lunch."

Erik and Mark had been friends with Jake since their toddler days. The threesome romped and played outdoors in every season. Erik often came up with the game plan. Mark played the jester, going along with the plan until he decided the game needed a little more zest. Jake, red-haired and fiery-cheeked, played as a friend to them both. He helped build the plot and elaborate on the scenario. He was as willing as Mark, however, to crash the game with a well-placed snowball or a wild wrestling match. It was easy to tell when their play had taken a turn toward silliness as Mark howled with huge convulsive laughter. Even Erik, often dismayed at his brother's irreverence, succumbed to Mark's bewitching humor.

Finally Mark got up from the table. He pulled on his boots and hollered, "See ya later, Mom!"

They stood in the doorway, the sun shining on a stair-step of blonde, then red, then darker, blonde hair. A familiar heaviness tugged at my chest, a homesickness borne when my two sons came into the world. As a result of becoming a mother, I'd flung open the doors of my soul. The birth of my sons suddenly seemed to offer a startling, new connection with God. More than ever before, I began to understand why God was considered a father, a parent. I realized what it meant to love someone who could give nothing back. Nothing except simply being. My babies taxed me with sleepless nights, soiled diapers, and ear infections. They demanded constant attention and unending energy. All the rigor that at one time was spent on education and career aspirations, now had to be quadrupled just to maintain a household. Some days it seemed enough just to survive without collapsing. And yet they delighted me, filled me at once with both rapture and despair. How would I ever manage to meet their constant needs or guide their emerging wills?

Every eyelash, finger, and toe of my children seemed to spring from the heart of God himself. Every giggle was a gift. Their cries tugged and tore at me, as though my own heart was breaking. Was it possible that God's capacity to love humanty—to love me—was greater even than my love for my own children? The idea was staggering.

"Be careful!" I said as the screen door slammed behind them. Once kids are old enough to play away from a parent's watchful gaze, "be careful" becomes a mantra of mother-hood. It is a fruitless thing to say, since "careful" seems beyond the vocabulary or comprehension of boys ages seven to seven-teen. Even so, mothers everywhere send fervent prayers we hope will wrap our children in a sheath of divine protection.

About an hour after the boys left to play at the creek, the phone rang.

Todd picked up the receiver.

"Hello."

Todd's eyes widened. His face grew ashen. He took a step as though to brace himself. "Is he dead?"

With those words, I realized that one of the boys was on the other line.

"Where is he?"

The cells of my body dissolved into liquid fear.

"Where are you? Okay, come on home."

Todd hung up and looked at me. "It's Mark. He's been run over."

I ran for the door. I didn't know exactly where to find Mark, but I knew which direction they had been playing. There was only one road they could cross on the way to the creek. As I reached for the door handle, Jake ran inside.

"Mark," he said, breathless, his blue eyes wild with fright. "He's hurt real bad."

I dashed out of the house and ran along the bike trail toward the road. Fear narrows the peripheral vision to a single focus, and mine was to get to my son. I narrowly caught sight of Erik coming out of a neighbor's house. He had come running home, but decided just two houses away to call us. Perhaps he thought a phone call would be faster. Or maybe he stopped to use a phone because he could not face us with the devastating news. In either case, as I ran by him I shouted, "Erik, where is he? Where is Mark?"

Erik pointed in the direction I was running. I flew along the trail, willing myself to get there before it was too late. Two things propelled me forward.

I did not want Mark to be alone.

And I had to tell him I loved him.

The wooded trail gave way to a paved street, where a navy blue pickup blocked the road at an angle. A crowd had started to form a circle around the other side of the vehicle. I tore around the front of the pickup. From somewhere I heard a man ask, "Are you his mother?"

I didn't respond. There, between the front and back wheels of the 4x4 pickup lay my son, limp and bleeding. He eyes were closed; his eyelashes pressed against bruised cheeks. I dropped to my knees and touched his face.

"My baby," I whispered. "Markie, I love you."

The rest of the world shrank away. I saw nothing but the broken body of my little boy, his limbs lying at odd angles against the dark asphalt pavement. He had been struck by the pickup. With brakes locked on steel-studded snow tires, the front right wheel of the pickup had skidded over his torso. I heard voices as if they came through a faraway tunnel. A man, apparently the driver, said, "I'm sorry. I'm so sorry." In the distance, Erik began to sob. Someone with a gentle voice spoke to him. Todd's voice asked, "Mark, where does it hurt?"

Blood flowed from Mark's nose and mouth. "Oh my God," Todd said. Pink fibrous clots lay splattered on the pavement around his head. It seemed that Mark's brain was leaking from a shattered skull. My face was next to Mark's, and as I kissed him I recognized the sour smell of vomit. The pink matter was the grapefruit he'd eaten for lunch.

"Markie," I said. "Can you hear me? I love you."

Mark opened his eyes and looked at me. He was very still. No crying or tears. No whimpers of pain.

Quietly, looking into my eyes, he asked, "Am I going to die?"

At his calm, sincere question my very soul poured out onto the pavement with him. Now all sounds and voices faded completely away.

"Of course not, honey," I said. *But I did not know.* I did not know how many moments remained for me to touch the face of my son and tell him how much I loved him. "Should we pray together, right now?"

"Yes," he said, and closed his eyes again.

"Dear God," I said, tears wetting my cheeks now for the

first time. "Please help Mark to be all right. Send Jesus to be with us. In his name we pray, Amen."

While these were the words I spoke aloud, inside I was shouting, pleading with God, *"Pour out the blood of your Son, Jesus, onto my son, Mark."*

I'd never prayed such a thing before. I didn't pray "Let him live, Lord." The words just cried out from some bottomless well of anguish. Maybe somehow I knew that, whether he lived or died, the power of Christ's blood was the only power big enough to save him. I don't know. But the moment I spoke the words to Mark, and shouted my plea through the vaults of the universe, I became calm. The space left after my being had emptied out onto the bloody pavement now flooded with an inexplicable peace. The scene around me expanded back into focus.

The paramedics were speaking to me loudly and clearly as though to a child. "Ma'am, we need you to move out of the way. We're here to help."

"I'll be right here, Markie. I love you."

The paramedics worked quickly yet carefully, sheltering Mark's body from further injury. They cut off his clothing, strongly suspecting a broken pelvis and spinal injuries. Mark groaned when they moved his arms, most probably broken. He groaned again when they lifted him to the litter. As they loaded Mark into the ambulance, Todd and I hugged each other. I leaned against his chest, glad for it and felt the tears come again. We trembled in each other's arms for a moment before breaking away. "I'll meet you at the hospital," Todd said.

I rode in the front seat of the ambulance, looking back at Mark through an opening between the seats.

"I'm right here, Mark." Two paramedics worked at once, hooking him up to IVs. Mark cried out as a medic wrapped a blood pressure cup around his arm. I was glad he protested, however feebly. I wanted him to keep making sounds, to keep his eyes open. Another medic taped an oxygen tube to his nose. I kept talking to Mark, not wanting to lose touch with him—as though communication itself was an umbilical cord between us, a lifeline until we could get to the hospital. The driver radioed into Anchorage. "Incoming. Male. Age eight. Vehicle pedestrian accident. Code blue."

We arrived and I followed the gurney into the emergency room. A nurse took me by the arm and explained that I would need to wait outside. I didn't want to leave Mark. That aching homesickness I'd felt earlier in the day was now a slashing wound. Yet I was grateful for the expertise of people whose job it was to piece together broken bodies. Reluctantly I let the nurse lead me away from the flurry of activity, assuring Mark I wouldn't be far away.

I sat in a small private waiting room with a phone. I leaned forward, my elbows against my legs, hands dangling between my knees. Again, I prayed, "God, please . . ." I remained calm, still enveloped in that remarkable sense of peace. I wondered why Todd wasn't there yet.

I picked up the phone to call Jake's mother, my friend Jane. In the aftermath of the accident, Jake walked back to our house, took off Mark's borrowed boots and placed them carefully, neatly next to the door. Then Jake called Jane and said, "I'm coming home." Jane picked him up walking bare-footed on the street just as police cordoned off the neighborhood from traffic. Todd spent thirty minutes looking for a traumatized red-haired little boy before realizing Jake had already made his way home. Once Jake's whereabouts were established and Erik was safely in the care of Jane's family, Todd headed for the hospital.

A doctor and nurse entered the waiting room and I quickly hung up the phone. The doctor explained that they were preparing Mark for a CAT scan to determine the extent of internal injuries, including brain and spinal damage. I nodded and the doctor left. The nurse stayed behind.

"Honey," she said, "let's go wash your hands."

I looked and noticed for the first time that my hands were crusted with Mark's blood. With one arm around my waist, she led me to a sink and turned on the water. Then she put soap on her own hands first and with gentle strokes washed my hands under a flow of cool water. I had not felt the slippery sensation of someone else's hands washing mine since my mother helped me wash as a very little girl. The feeling was both intimate and comforting—an act of tender mercy.

I accompanied Mark from the CAT scan to the X-ray room, where doctors checked his arms and pelvis for fractures. The pediatric surgeon arrived, wanting to know what had happened. His deep quiet voice, practiced in countless encounters with distraught parents, was an antidote to panic. Yet when I explained that the wheel of a pickup had skidded over Mark's abdomen, he touched his hand to his temple and grimaced. He was ready to scrub for surgery but it was evident that his expectations were grim. Mark, overhearing me talk to the doctor, asked, "What, Mom? I got run over?"

Although Mark had been conscious throughout the ordeal, he was now for the first time aware of his surroundings. He did not remember what happened. Todd arrived during the X-rays. He explained his delay and I explained what the doctors had done so far. We didn't have long to wait for the doctor's verdict. The pediatric surgeon and the emergency room doctor called us into the X-ray room where they were examining thirty or more X-rays.

"Can you explain again exactly what happened?" the ER doctor asked.

We told the story again, confirming what Erik, Jake, and eyewitnesses had told police and Todd. The boys had been walking home when Mark threw a snowball, instigating a game of tag. Mark, taunting and laughing his laugh, ran ahead with Erik and Jake in hot pursuit. Not noticing the trail's intersection with the street, Mark dashed out in front of an oncoming pickup truck. There was time only for the driver to slam on the brake before the truck's front bumper struck Mark down. Then the wheel of a full-size 4x4 pickup with metal-studded snow tires skidded on dry pavement over Mark's body.

The doctors looked at each other and shook their heads. The surgeon said, "Your son is one lucky boy. It appears he has no internal injuries. He has no broken bones. His skull, spine, and brain are all intact. He's got some lacerations inside his mouth, but we won't even stitch it up. It'll heal on its own. Except for bruises and abrasions, it looks like he'll be okay."

Todd and I looked at each other, incredulous.

"There's no explaining it," said the ER doctor. "Sometimes miracles happen." They decided to keep Mark in the hospital for a few days, to make sure they hadn't missed something, and in the days that followed, nurses and staff stopped in to say hello to the boy whose unlikely story had made big news throughout the hospital.

Relief, gratitude, and awe washed over me, filling me with a strange lightness of being—an expansion of the peace I'd felt as I knelt on the street with my bleeding son. Todd and I sat down in a chair together next to Mark's bed as he slept.

We wrapped our arms around each other. Then we both began to weep with deep choking sobs. Mark, who by all the natural laws of physics should be dead, was in fact alive, his skin warm to the touch, his eyelids flickering in sleep. He would come home to us after all. Tears spilled unrestrained down our faces. We were overwhelmed by this gift of life, a wonder that surpassed even the miracle of Mark's birth, when we had held each other in a delivery room and cried tears of joy. I had glimpsed in a new unfathomable way, the mystery of the word "resurrection."

Mark was so sore he could hardly move the next morning. Both eyes had swollen nearly shut. Dried blood filled a deep crack in his lip. Abrasions on his arms and hip glistened with rawness. It was another full day before he could get out of bed, and weeks before the shadowed evidence of his accident fully left his body.

In his hospital room, as he gingerly sipped Seven-Up through a straw, I asked Mark if he remembered anything about what had happened.

"I just remember one thing," he said, his darkly bruised eyes misting with tears. "I just remember that you prayed, Mom. You prayed for me."

PORCUPINE PROMISES

My resolve and the boys' promise lasted roughly three weeks. I could not keep my sons from exploring any more than I could keep them from sleeping at night or waking up in the morning. Although I insisted that they stay within the agreed boundaries, I could not enforce my edict.

The boys were nine and eleven years old, an age of adventure and growing independence. All summer they played in the woods along the edge of town, climbing trees, building forts, and enacting heroic quests.

One day Mark sidled up to me in that way he had of testing my reaction to what he was about to say. Erik stood to the side, preoccupied enough to appear innocent but close enough to listen to my response. They were a team, those two.

"We found a cave," Mark said, his voice measured but his dark blue eyes betraying his excitement.

"Where?" I asked.

"Just past the second rock face," he answered, glancing at his brother.

"That's past your boundary, Mark," I answered. "You guys know not to go past those rocks." Everything beyond was steep, rugged terrain.

The boys had been graduating from one "wild" place to the next from the time they were toddlers. First they played in our backyard. A fenced area with a little wooded hill, it was covered with low-bush cranberries, a few climbing trees, and spindly young alders. With the boys bundled into snowsuits, the hill provided a gentle place to sled in the winter. Within a year or so the cranberries had been consumed and the plants trampled underfoot. The trees had become as familiar as an old shoe, and the hill seemed little more than a mound. The boys' imaginations had excavated every would-be adventure of their enclosure.

The neighbor's empty lot, on the other hand, had grand possibilities. More trees. Less supervision. And no fences. We called the place "Jeanie's Woods," after our neighbor who owned the lot. The distance from home was exciting, a place out of earshot and just beyond my watchful eye. Here in this half-acre wilderness, a neighbor boy first taught the boys to swear. Their progression from our backyard to Jeanie's Woods and beyond was the subject of long negotiations and longer lists of rules about what they were allowed to do while adventuring in new places. The second rock face was their current imposed limit and the cave Mark was talking about lay well beyond it.

"Mom, come look at it with us. It's really cool," Mark said.

I looked at Erik and he nodded his complicity. "It's awesome," Erik said. "But we made sure it's safe. We tied a rope to a strong tree."

"Why would you need a rope?" I asked, alarmed.

Alarm. It was becoming a familiar sensation growing in proportion to the boys' independence. It was a jumpy feeling—an uneasy sense of dangling somewhere between the freedom of the hills and the fear of what could happen there.

I decided to see what the boys were talking about, if for no other reason than to forbid this newfound danger. It was a familiar routine—my checking out new places and drawing fresh borders around the areas they could explore.

My longtime friend Jane, Jake's mother, came along and we followed the boys through the woods. Jane understood my conflict. Jake and my boys often explored together. Jane and I both cherished wild places and yet mistrusted the fickle judgment of a nine-year-old. The trail meandered through alder, scrub willow, and high-bush cranberries. We kept our eyes open for moose that often foraged along the hillside. Wildlife encounters were both a hazard and a thrill. A human's approach usually sent moose crashing away like bulldozers through the forest. Other times, a mother moose with a calf stood her ground, forcing hikers to back down the trail. Spring bears, lean and cranky from long winter naps, also rambled through the hills nearby. I kept these and other dangers in some semiconscious corner of my mind—refusing to wake to them completely for fear that a hard look would keep us from fully experiencing all that this landscape had to offer.

After hiking uphill for a distance, we stopped to catch our breath at the first rock face; a place that had at one time marked the furthest reaches of the boys' frontier. The trail to the second rock face was virtually nonexistent. The boys simply followed one landmark after another like a dot-to-dot puzzle, first the double-trunked spruce tree, then the fallen birch, on through the tall grass and to the left. While the first rock face was a simple outcropping of boulders, this wall of granite jutted twenty feet above us. The boys climbed around it, scrambling like mountain goats to the top of its wide plateau. They looked down at us with jubilation.

"Come on you guys!" Erik said. "It's great up here."

Jane and I looked at each other. She must have wondered when I would say we'd come far enough—when it was time to go home.

"How much further to the cave?" I asked.

"Not far," the boys assured us.

Fifty yards above the timberline, we could see all of Eagle River Valley below us. We picked out our house, the red, metal roof of the school, and the bubbles of greenhouses at the nursery down the road. Still the cave was above us. The boys led us to a three-foot-wide crevice in another twenty-foot wall of granite. There was no climbing around it. A nylon rope hung from over the lip of the fissure.

"Grab the rope and use the sides of the rocks to climb up," Mark said.

Cavalier and confident, the boys shimmied to the top. "It's totally safe, Mom," Erik said. "The rope is tied to a really strong tree up here. I've tested it."

Part of me burned with anger at how far beyond my limits the boys had wandered without permission. Yet grudgingly I admired their nerve.

One at a time I and then Jane climbed up behind the boys only to find that the rope was fastened tenuously to a tiny shrub. There are, after all, no trees above timberline. At this point, Jane, a wise woman, sat down. "I'll meet you guys on your way back," she said, friendly but resolute.

From there I followed the boys across a steep slant of loose shale. Still, I did not say "no." I did not insist on turning back. All that remained of my maternal sensibilities stayed behind, keeping company with a friend who was growing smaller in the distance. In an unspoken apology at abandoning her, my last echo of rationalization was this: "Better to hang out in the mountains than at the mall."

Suddenly I grew eager to see the cave. The air seemed to crackle with exhilaration—a giddy, unleashed sense of joy. The cave was just a bit further, the boys assured me. At that moment I would have followed them anywhere. I had become Sam Gribley, the runaway character of *My Side of the Mountain*. Only this was far better than the book—with the fine company of like-minded friends who didn't mind getting dirty or taking chances. I realized that the cave we were looking for was the one whose opening we could see among the cliffs from our backyard deck—the one we speculated was big enough to live in.

A thin shelf of granite was all that remained before reaching the cave. The ground below the ledge angled steeply toward the edge of a vertical drop-off. Erik scooted around the ledge first, stepping gingerly around the curve of a boulder until he reached the cave's entrance. Mark went next. He spread his arms, hugging the boulder for balance.

Just as Mark inched out of my reach, a wasp landed lightly on his outstretched hand. At the same moment, Erik dislodged a large rock sending it crashing down the mountainside like a rough-edged cannon. My euphoria evaporated. A scene unfolded instantly before me—if that wasp stung Mark, he would lose his balance and tumble down the mountain. Only Mark was no rock; he would be rag-doll soft and utterly irretrievable.

Fear filled my mouth. A sick dread welled up like the taste of a nightmare, reminiscent of the scene of Mark's accident, and for an instant my arms and legs grew wooden. I could hardly breathe. In the echo of the crash, a trickle of rocks skittered down the mountainside. Suddenly the dread vanished, replaced by a surge of primal, maternal rage. My consent to this expedition seemed utterly outrageous. What had I been thinking?

The wasp flew away without Mark's notice and he made it safely around the boulder to the entrance of the cave. The opening was just big enough for the boys to sit together, side by side, just big enough for a porcupine. I tiptoed shakily around the same narrow ledge and stood on the shelf that jutted just shoulder width from the cave's entrance. A wisp of hair blew gently across Erik's smiling face. Mark's eyes shone with pride. I tried to maintain my composure. Erik crawled inside the cave then quickly backed out with a fist full of old quills a porcupine had left behind.

"Isn't this cool?"

Once I found my voice, once the thought of a broken child lying at the bottom of the mountain subsided, harsh words shot out of my mouth.

"Are you both out of your minds?" I shouted. "Do you know how far past your boundaries this is?"

A look of confusion registered on the boy's faces. Hadn't we just been enjoying ourselves?

I continued. "You guys are both grounded. What were you thinking, coming all the way up here? Look at that rock that just fell down—what if that had been you?"

I announced it was time to go home. Never were the boys to return to this place.

The boys, stunned, looked at me like bear cubs whose mother had pressed her teeth against their tender necks in grim warning.

Then Mark grew indignant. "We know what we're doing, Mom." Erik glowered, his silent anger burning quietly behind narrowed eyes.

I cut them off, closing off any further retort. In my lapse between being a mother and a storybook character, sinister possibilities had presented themselves—a dark image of disaster. Unless they agreed never to return here, they would not be allowed to play even in the woods closest to home. I made them promise it—never again.

How oddly I was jolted between the magnetic draw of the wild and raw maternal instinct. I walked a high-voltage tightrope as I balanced the boys' adventure-filled childhood—one I had only dreamed about living—with my concern for their safety. Ultimately, it would have been safer to stay at home and play video games. But we lived in Alaska for a more soulfull existence. Wild places had more to teach about life and love and Creation than anything else I could imagine. And so

I walked that tightrope one step at a time, hoping I would not fall or fail them.

The rigors of this balancing act were offset by something else. All the time that I was inching along that narrow cable, I really yearned for the thrill of the trapeze. I wanted to fly. Like a hawk launching from the edge of a cliff, I wanted to defy gravity and leave the fear of it behind. While I could accept my own mortality and weigh the risks against it, I was inextricably connected to human sons whose fragility terrified me. Gravity could send them tumbling from the mouth of a cave into the jaws of a ravine. And with them would vanish my grip on anything of beauty or consequence or hope.

The birth of my sons had somehow transformed my experience of the natural wonders of the world. They were, after all, each a wonder unto himself—the very mysteries of the universe seemed wrapped up in their humanity. Now the white waters of clear mountain streams, the heavens on a starlit winter night, the glow of a morning sunrise were made more meaningful because I shared it with two little boys who were seeing it all for the first time. They became the lens through which to see all things beautiful and worthy. All joy seemed to flow from the context of their lives. Without them the world would surely grow parched.

So I forced the boys to make promises they could not keep.

The contradiction, of course, was my desire for them to discover the exhilaration of wild places. In their wilderness endeavors surely they would grow nearer to the heart of God. The expansive dome of sky, the sculpted earth, the ebb and flow of seasons—all pointed to a Being who had the power to set their spirits free. While every terror on their behalf was followed by the resolve, "Never again," my will was easily eroded by a wordless call to some truer side of the mountain.

A month or so after the cave incident, the boys announced they had found a new trail to the river. Yes, it was a little past their boundaries in that direction. It wasn't that far—really. I looked at my sons, their faces radiant with anticipation.

"Show me," I said.

SYMPHONY LAKE

Ice chimes.

I listen for them still, years after their brittle memory
has faded into that cobwebbed treasure box of past loves and
longing. I suppose it was the beginning of good-byes, the
beginning of the boys' journeys away in ships of their own making. For some time, it seemed that I stood on a shore watching
as the vessels of their lives grew smaller in the distance, wondering how long before they would disappear on the horizon.

The jewel of Symphony Lake lay at the foot of Cantata and
Triangle Peaks. Calliope Mountain rose just behind the Peaks,
forming a geologic trinity that towered over the south fork of
Eagle River Valley. Snow runoff from these mountains fed
Symphony Lake, which was a depository for the deep blue
transparency of sky. A second lake, a gem of a different color,

lay across a narrow isthmus from Symphony Lake. Fed by the silty runoff of Flute Glacier, the waters of Eagle Lake were a milky, aqua green. Side by side, the two lakes formed a sparkling pendant at the base of the mountain's spires. It was here that Mark and his friends wanted to camp.

Mark, now a thirteen-year-old, came home after school on a fall Friday with a plan. Anticipating my objections he'd already collected permission from the parents of several friends whom he'd invited to the campout. He'd even managed to arrange a ride to the trailhead. If I was really worried about bears, he would carry my revolver. Would I pick them up the next day?

The only way into the area was a six-mile hike along the valley floor. Like all Alaskan backcountry destinations, the hike held the possibility of wildlife encounters. Moose, marmot, bears, and Dall sheep all lived in the valley's cradle. Wildlife was only one of my concerns for the boys. Would their good sense and outdoor skills override boyish temptations to jump into the frigid lakes, climb the rocky spires, or cook bear-attracting food near their tents? As usual, Mark's destination was a long way past the boundaries of where I allowed the boys to camp on their own. And again, my first inclination was to say, "No."

I had just hiked the trail earlier in the week. The tundra was ablaze with color. Crowberry and cranberry leaves burned red across the alpine slopes. Lower in the valley, birch and aspen trees glowed as if each leaf held a fleck of yellow sun. The cool air made my nose run and added to our dog's exuberance. I thought about the musical names of the area's geologic features—Harp Mountain, Flute and Organ Glaciers—and thought about how the day itself felt like a song. I was especially struck by one thing—the overwhelming appeal of an overnight campout at the lakes.

Mark had a good-sized group going, four other boys his age. What more could go wrong at Symphony Lake than anywhere else the boys were allowed to camp? Given my earlier hike, how could I say no? Yes, I would pick them up the next day. But absolutely no gun, even if Mark had proven himself in a hunter safety course. The bear pepper spray would have to suffice.

"Bring an extra-warm sleeping bag," I said. Temperatures at night had begun to dip below freezing. I could not keep myself from issuing parental directives, one after the other. "Don't forget the cell phone." We all knew the cell phone didn't work that far back in the valley. My rationale was that, in an emergency, someone would hike high enough on a ridge for the phone to pick up a signal.

Mark packed his gear, whistling as he stuffed his tent, sleeping bag, and the dubious cell phone into a backpack. My litany of warnings and requirements were, I imagine, little more than a faint, persistent murmur in the background of his enthusiastic preparations.

As I watched him pack, I remembered the first backpack I had given him and Erik. Mark was almost two years old; Erik was three. We had just moved to Alaska and were eager to get outdoors—but not before I'd given them a lesson in outdoor survival.

I presented each a blue dinosaur backpack and invited them to take out, one by one, the items that made up their "survival" gear. As they did, I explained each article. They could use the small signaling mirror to shine at any aircraft flying overhead. (We actually practiced this.) The whistle was to signal people searching on the ground—the human voice tires easily and is drowned out by other sounds. A foil emergency blanket and hand warmers would help them stay warm until help arrived. Each pack also carried a candy bar, a canteen, and a compass. We had no idea how to use a compass, but a survival pack hardly seemed complete without one.

"If you ever get lost, find a tree and make it your friend," I said. "Stay with the tree until someone finds you. Don't wander, or you'll get even more lost. Someone will be looking for you."

Mark's round eyes absorbed my words with great solemnity. Erik listened intently with his hands clasped in his lap.

At the end of my serious talk, they grinned at each other and repacked their new wares. I had just handed them their invincibility. At two and three years old, they were ready to tackle the world. They squared their shoulders and headed for the wilds of our fenced backyard to rehearse getting lost. Half an hour later, Erik came inside, with a pressing question—his brother following close behind.

"Can we practice eating the candy bar?" he asked.

"It's an emoogency," Mark, said. Chocolate already rimmed the edge of his mouth.

Now Mark stood broad-shouldered, nearly six feet tall and ready for real adventure. He stuffed in an extra package of beef jerky and zipped his pack closed. Both he and Erik were Boy Scouts long enough to learn the outdoor skills they needed, take a few supervised trips, and accumulate their gear. But they had no patience for earning badges or the formality of progression through the ranks. They wanted only to put those skills to work—to go camping, climbing, exploring. The boys' brief Scouting experience did develop their confidence and they managed to convince their friend's and their friends' parents of their extreme competence in the wild. It amazed me how readily parents allowed their sons to accompany mine as they tromped around Eagle River Valley. Among my admonitions to the boys, then, was the responsibility they held toward their less experienced friends.

Someone honked the horn outside, and Mark grabbed his pack to go. He stood at the doorway and paused.

Recently Mark found it awkward to participate in our casual, customary hugs of departure. Even so, he occasionally still sat on my lap after dinner, his long legs draped over mine, his arm wrapped around my shoulders. He still smelled like a puppy, like dirt and rain. On the periphery of his boyish scent immerged the faint hint of manly sweat.

"Have a good time, Mark," I said. "Be careful."

He shifted on his feet, struggling with some decision. Then he raised his hand, placed it on top my head—as if to bless me—and said, "Good-bye."

I wondered, as the car pulled out of the driveway, if I'd emphasized quite enough, my directive not to attempt the peaks around the Eagle and Symphony lakes. Had they promised not to climb?

Then I remembered my own promises, those attempts to appease my parents and ease their anxiety.

"Where's Kaylene?" my mother had asked, frantic at my disappearance.

"Typical," my dad grumbled, his face darkening with anger not because I went missing again—he knew I'd turn up—but that I should cause my mother such distress. Too often family outings grew tense and unhappy because I wandered out of earshot. I couldn't seem to help myself. I knew the trouble I'd face upon my return. And yet, to adventure alone without the worried fussing of adults or the squabble of siblings proved irresistible every time. To hear no sound except the chirp of birds, the scurry of a mouse, and the song of crickets made me wonder what it would be like to live as a deer in the woods. I tried to walk without breaking twigs or crunching leaves. I imagined I was a deer. I would live here near this tiny gurgle of a stream. And I would eat from the grassy meadow over there. In a storm, I would hide under the outcropping of this rock shelf. Oh, and look here are fossils! And I would load my pockets with the imprint of leaves on red scoria.

I was never lost.

Eventually my musings were interrupted by the frantic call of parents. Reluctantly I returned to the storm of their indignation and relief. I was made to promise that I would never, ever wander so far again. That I would always let mom and dad know where I was going, that I would never again go alone. With eyes lowered, my throat aching with tears, I promised.

And I lied.

How many of those same sorts of promises was I extorting from Erik and Mark these days? I grew annoyed listening to my demands for guarantees that the boys never venture beyond the sound of my voice, or at the least, the echo of my conscience. I threatened consequences. Promises were my contracts for control. Yet, just as I could not help myself from wandering away from my parents' watchful eye as a child, I could not seem to keep from coercing my sons into making promises they could not keep.

That night as I lay in bed, I prayed for Mark and his friends' safety and good sense. I prayed that wildlife would stay away and the weather wouldn't get too cold. Prayer was now a stay against the unknown. As I nodded off, adrift in those translucent colors between sleep and wakefulness, I heard the sound of boys' laughter echoing through a valley. And wistfulness, like cool silk, slid through the dream.

I picked the boys up at the trailhead with a warm car, a dozen donuts, and a jug of orange juice. They piled in and plowed into the goodies while I quizzed them about their trip. Yes, they'd seen a huge bull moose, on the opposite side of the river. No, they hadn't seen any bears. They'd also discovered some overflow ponds around the lake that were frozen enough to slide across.

"The water was so clear, you couldn't tell at first that it was even frozen," Mark said. "I suppose it was ten feet deep. We could see straight to the bottom." They talked about this the rest of the ten-mile drive home. They felt suspended on the clear ice like hovercrafts above the bouldered bottom of the pond. I bit my lip to keep from reprimanding the boys for what sounded like reckless behavior on thin ice. They were all back safe, after all.

We dropped off Mark's friends. With the car empty now, Mark had more he wanted to tell me about their trip.

"It was so freaky, Mom," he said. "I woke up in the middle of the night and couldn't sleep. The wind had come up and there was this weird sound."

He paused, and in the silence I could only imagine a bear snuffling through his pack. Why did my mind fixate on the most frightful thing I could think of? I held my breath, waiting to hear more.

"It was this tinkling noise." His voice lowered with a sense of awe. "The wind made waves and broke up the ice frozen around the edge of the lake. What I heard were shards of ice clinking against each other."

We looked into each other's faces. Mark's eyes reflected a deep well of wonder, and I drank from it. It was a new taste, a bittersweet regret at having missed something so amazing, and yet the joy of living it vicariously, through the words of my son.

"So, what exactly did it sound like?" I asked. In all the years I had camped or backpacked I had never even heard of this phenomenon. The conditions of that night, the cold, the wind, the temperature of the lake had all converged to create a shore-side concert, music I could only imagine.

"Ice chimes," Mark said. "It sounded like ice chimes."

It was not the first time, nor would it be the last that Mark or Erik came home to tell me about their experiences in the wilderness. But the ethereal sound of nature singing through a choir of crystal marked a turning point—yet another shift in the landscape of our relationship. Too soon, it seemed, the trails they took would extend beyond the map of my world—and I would have to be content to hear their stories of distant places.

I hiked back to Symphony Lake after Mark's camping trip and stood on the isthmus between Symphony and Eagle lakes. The water around the edges was frozen now; the open circles in the middle of the lakes had slowly sealed closed for the winter. There was no longer any chance of hearing ice chimes this season. Clouds shrouded the tops of Cantata, Calliope, and Triangle peaks. Patches of blue sky peered intermittently between their jagged crests. The clean smell of snow hung in the air. Here I was, breaking the very rules I had made the boys promise to keep, hiking alone in wild country.

I knew before venturing out, the unlikelihood of recapturing Mark's experience. It was his gift, not mine. Standing at the edge of the frozen water, an edgy sense of impending change seeped into my bones. With that odd awareness of twilight, I knew darker days would soon consume our abundant season of light. And while it all reflected the natural phases of earth and sky, sun and stars, I could not help feeling a little sad.

I shivered at the bitter breeze and knew I should head for home. I needed to move on to stay warm. To survive the coming winter.

Faith Falls

Primrose Creek cascades into Porcupine Creek in a 100-foot drop of white, churning water. The water rages over a wall of granite before crashing into a boulder-strewn gorge where Porcupine Creek cuts a crease into the mountain's flank. We would never have discovered the falls except that deep snow on the trail kept us from reaching our original destination of Lost Lake.

Erik and Mark and I—along with my friend Jane and her son, Jake—began our backpacking trip at the Primrose Trailhead on a sunny day in June. The forest near the coastal waters of Resurrection Bay had a fairy-tale quality compared to the drier black spruce forests closer to home in Eagle River. Here, light filtered through a gossamer veil of lichen that draped over the arms of up-reaching trees. Soft, green moss clung to the thick trunks of white spruce and hemlock. Young ferns were beginning to fan open on sunnier sections of the trail. Shoots of false hellebore pushed up through the ground like green bananas. It wouldn't be long, in the nearly round-the-clock daylight, before this plant spread its enormous leaves to the sun.

The boys walked ahead while Jane and I followed, reminiscing about other outdoor outings we'd taken together when our children were much younger. We had been friends now for eleven years and people we met often asked if we were sisters. We were both tall, fair-skinned, with shoulder-length hair. Beyond this, I wondered if our faces shared a certain amalgam of fond bewilderment, an expression peculiar to mothers with sons.

Mark, at thirteen, was tall and skinny with a mirthful grin that still revealed little-boy dimples. As the boys walked three abreast, Mark occasionally bumped into his brother just to knock him off balance. Given to forgetful daydreaming, Erik, at fifteen, took it in stride, dodged Mark when he could and occasionally stumbled over an untied bootlace. Jake, just between them in age, laughed at their antics. Jake's rosy cheeks had grown from the round softness of childhood to an angular glimmer of a young adult. The only person missing from the picture was Jane's sixteen-year-old-daughter, who had recently discovered interests outside those of her brother and his smelly friends.

Both Janes' husband and mine worked demanding schedules with long stretches spent away from home. And the time they did have off was often dedicated to hunting or fishing. So while the kids were still toddlers, without any particular deliberation, we formed an alliance. On days off from our own jobs and school, we took the kids adventuring. In the light of Jane's sense of humor and gentle wisdom, life felt less frazzled. She had a knack for listening that helped smooth the rumpled fabric of family life. Frustrations seemed more bearable when they were shared.

So she understood, as we hiked and talked, my wistfulness about Erik's recent decision. A year earlier, Todd and I had presented Erik a leather-bound Bible with his name embossed in gold letters. Confirmation marked his passage into an adult faith, the beginning of a personal accountability to God. The Bible was a keepsake that I hoped would attend all of life's important events—his graduation, his marriage, and the birth of his children. I imagined the worn leather in my son's aging hands as he drew comfort from its words during the twilight of his life.

But just a few days before this backpacking trip, Erik had given the Bible to a youngster in the Alaska Native village of Copper Center. It was Erik's going-away gift to a sad-eyed boy, one of the many children ages three to thirteen who'd attended the Vacation Bible School put on by our church youth group. The youth group called itself F.I.S.H.—an acronym for Faith,

Integrity, Service, Honor. When I arrived to drive them home at the end of the week, weeping children hung on to Erik's arms and clung to his legs, begging him and the others not to leave. At home, Erik told me about Benjamin. And as warmed as I was by Erik's bigheartedness, I'd swallowed hard when he told me his Bible now belonged to someone else.

Jane listened quietly. As we climbed, dirty patches of snow stretched across shadowed sections of the muddy trail. Jane had little use for organized religion. Although she claimed not to believe in God or church, she did believe in kindness. She recognized Erik's generosity as an act of faith both childlike and wise.

As we talked, I discovered the distinct outline of a bear's paw on the soft trail. I kneeled to inspect the impression. The edges of the track were clear and still damp. We called to the boys and realized that although we'd agreed to hike together, they had gone on ahead, quite beyond our sight and hearing. We picked up our pace to catch them. A little farther along lay a fresh pile of bear scat. Jane and I looked at each other and kept moving. It took another half hour of uphill climbing before we reached the boys—who had shed their packs for a snowball fight. We reminded them of our agreement to stay close together.

"Fine," they said.

Within fifteen minutes they again were half a mile ahead of us.

We greeted a young couple hiking the other direction on the trail and asked if they had seen the boys. Yes, they had passed them at the abandoned mine about halfway to the lake. Lost Lake, they said, was still frozen. Our fly-fishing rods would be of no use on this trip.

We met up with the boys at the mine, an open area that overlooked the blue waters of the Kenai Lake below. Jake and Mark used sticks to whack on the dry hollow stems of last year's cow parsnip, sending splinters of dead plants flying. Erik, wearing a crusty old hard hat he'd found half-buried in the ground, peeked out the window of a dilapidated cabin. I was reluctant to scold the boys. They were having so much fun, playing as they had when they were little. In not so many years, we would no longer being doing this together. I wanted to make a happy memory.

"What's the deal?" I asked. "I thought we agreed you wouldn't get so far ahead."

"It's not our fault that you guys are so slow," Mark said, taking another swipe at the cow parsnip. Jake and Erik nodded their agreement.

"Listen," I said. "There are bears in the area. Either we stay together or we turn around and go back."

Resentment crept across the boys' faces. Erik set his mouth in an angry line. Mark's brow furrowed into a frown. Jake rolled his eyes. And I sensed that something about this backpacking trip was different. We had left behind daily routine for the soulful embrace of the backcountry. But along with their enthusiasm, the boys had brought with them the creeping shadow of adolescent disdain.

Soft snow buried the trail beyond the mine, making the path to Lost Lake nearly impassible. Since we couldn't fly-fish, we decided to go back and camp at the waterfall the boys had discovered earlier.

Although the sound of melting snow trickled all around us, at a certain point on the trail we could hear the faint roar of white water. Somehow, in our earlier hurry to catch up, Jane and I had missed this. The boys bounded off the trail toward the sound. We climbed over logs, ducked under fallen trees, and generally bushwhacked about a quarter of a mile before reaching the edge of a ravine that overlooked Porcupine Creek. Primrose Creek gushed over the opposite side of the canyon, spilling into the water below in a cascade of thundering power. At the base of the 100-foot falls, a house-sized rock reached up to receive the rush of water like a cupped hand. White rivulets streamed between its glossy black fingers.

This was what I loved about the backcountry—the possibility of discovery. When the senses feast on what nature has to offer, the spirit expands to receive not only beauty, but the power of revelation. It seemed to me that the whole purpose of creation was to reflect the nature of God.

Jane and I dug out our cameras to take pictures.

"I wonder if this place has a name," Erik said. As always when he grew thoughtful, his blue eyes narrowed and his head tilted slightly. "Let's call it Faith Falls. I'm going to name all the places I find this summer after FISH. This will be Faith Falls. I'll call the next place Integrity peak or creek—whatever it happens to be."

It was true that this waterfall had no known name. A natural falls of this caliber would have been a national monument anywhere else. But in Alaska, naming every stream, waterfall, or mountain was like naming the stars. After a while you run out of ideas. There were already 105 places in Alaska—coves, rivers, bays, mountains, and creeks—with the word "Eagle" in the name. The number of "Fish" creeks, lakes, mountains, points, and bays was endless. So "Faith Falls" seemed like a perfectly reasonable thing to call this place.

How interesting that Erik—like Adam naming the animals of Eden—wanted to name these places, wanted to lay claim to them in some way. Before Jane and I put our cameras away, the boys posed "GQ" style, making us laugh. With faraway looks and come-hither postures, they said, "Yes. We're cool." Mark stripped off his shirt, curled his arms, and tightened his stomach. He didn't realize that masculine bravado along with his knobby knees and stick-legs emerging from clunky hiking boots made him look like a scrawny, big-pawed puppy.

We agreed this was a good place to camp. But we would have to be especially vigilant about bears. The sound of the falls kept us from hearing anything except our raised voices. A clean camp was a must. We decided to fix dinner and then find a way down to the water. We each cooked our own meal—an arrangement that suited everyone. The kids could have their autonomy and Jane and I gladly shed any vestiges of domesticity. Besides, the boys claimed to be competent outdoorsmen and decent cooks. We arranged a camp kitchen in the clearing overlooking the ravine. The boys pulled their one-burner mountaineering stoves from their packs along with boxes of macaroni and cheese.

Jane and I were immersed in preparing our own pasta dinner, when suddenly the guys let out a whoop. We looked up to see a circle of fire burning on the ground around Mark's camp stove. The boys were laughing. Jake clutched his sides with hilarity.

Jane and I grabbed our water bottles as Mark began stomping out the flames. He quickly quelled the fire, but Jane and I looked at each other, wondering about the competence of these outdoorsmen. Mark had apparently spilled a good portion of his fuel on the ground before striking a match to light the stove.

"Geez, Mark. You could have lit the whole side of the mountain on fire. What were you thinking?" I asked.

Mark rolled his eyes. "Chill out, Mom. I know what I'm doing."

I clenched my teeth. The last thing I wanted on this outing was conflict and confrontation. I took a deep breath and swallowed. Anger settled like a hot stone in my stomach. At some point during the trip he would need more fuel, presumably from me. Surely he had learned from his mistake— he just wouldn't admit it.

After dinner the boys headed for the canyon bottom to look for a place to fish. Clouds had turned the blue sky into a smooth slate of gray. Jane and I decided to pitch a tent in case it began to rain. We placed a tent 100 yards away from the camp kitchen. Carefully we hung our remaining food from a tree a good 100 yards in the opposite direction. As old friends we seemed to know each other's mind— a different thing than thinking alike—and we worked together with easy deliberation.

We were returning from our food cache when we discovered a teenage dumping ground. Their backpacks were strewn carelessly across the ground just as they had left them. Candy bars and peanuts spilled out of open compartments. Dirty dishes from dinner rested against the mossy forest floor. Pieces of their tent lay scattered. The only thing missing was a sign that said "Bears Welcome." Just then rain began to patter softly against their open packs.

With hardly a word, Jane and I began to collect their

things. So much for relinquishing our roles as caretakers. Here we were, picking up after our sons. My resolve to avoid conflict dissolved with the rain. On the one hand the boys wanted to be expedition leaders without any parental directives. Yet here lay evidence that they had survived all those unsupervised experiences only by grace and good luck.

After tucking their things away, Jane and I decided to do a little exploring of our own, making our way down a steep embankment toward the falls. We scooted much of the way, knowing it would be a hefty climb to get back. The rain had stopped as quickly as it began but not without first releasing the scent of spring, a deep green smell of wet dirt and sunshine. I inhaled the forest's perfume. Clutching at the soft cool moss, we descended on heels and hands into the canyon. Anger seemed so inconsequential here, a small human fist against the broad night sky. As we approached the boulder-strewn stream, a cold mist from the falls dissipated my last burn of anger. To be truly present in this moment was enough.

The next morning the boys woke up eager to return to the stream and the falls. The tongue-lashing they'd received after we'd all returned to camp last night had been met with predictable contempt. But this was a new day. A new page to write a happier story. They dressed and headed toward the water. Jane and I sipped on hot coffee as the sun crested the mountains and poured into the clearing.

We talked about whether to stay another night or backpack somewhere else, and decided to ask the guys their preference. I leaned against a tree and closed my eyes to the warming sun. It wasn't long before Erik and Jake galloped into camp grinning, their heads dripping wet.

"You've got to come see this, Mom," Jake said. "There's the coolest place to wash your hair."

We laughed. It was as though they'd waited all their lives to find such a place.

"Where's Mark?" I asked.

"I dunno," Erik said. "He was right behind us."

We waited a few moments, but Mark didn't show. Jane suggested she and the boys backtrack the same way they'd come. I would wait in case Mark found his way to camp. As I watched Jane and Jake and Erik head down the canyon, my worry and frustration melded into a single sentiment. Rage. Suddenly I did not want to be backpacking with my sons. I was cursed with knowledge. To know the fallibility of their judgment was to lose faith in them and in an upbringing that underscored respect for surroundings far more powerful than they. I didn't want to be afraid for them any longer. I simply did not want to know. Yet I *did* know and I was afraid and the fact of it filled me with fury. How dare they rob from me the joy of this outing? Their provocations tore at the fabric of the connections I so wanted to weave with them here in the wilderness. And in the moment that I no longer wanted to share in this adventure—in perhaps any adventure ever again—it seemed that something between us was lost.

Mark marched into camp and put his hands on his hips. My relief at seeing him blazed only briefly in the firestorm of my anger.

"Where have you been?" he demanded.

"What do you mean, where have I been?" I asked. "Where were you?"

I thundered at him for every frustration that had ever passed between us. He yelled back. Cocky. Insolent.

"Why did you even come on this backpacking trip?" Mark asked. "We'd have more fun without you."

"That may be," I said. "But you can forget about going out on your own again if you don't take better care of your camp and each other." Then I listed the boys' safety blunders so far: not staying together as we hiked; lighting the forest floor on fire; inviting bears into a dirty camp; and now losing track of each other. Had they completely lost all semblance of common sense? Mark dismissed every accusation.

"That's ridiculous," he said, his jaw set with arrogant confidence. That anyone could be so profoundly sure of himself and so profoundly wrong amazed me.

Red-faced and angry, we finally grew silent with the same conclusion. On the next backpacking trip we would go *without* the other. The roar of water filled the empty space between us.

"Come on let's go. The others are waiting," I said. Mark led the way.

As we descended into the ravine, I paused to look at the waterfall across the canyon's divide. For better or worse, my sons were now making decisions on their own—unexpected and beyond my control. Some of their choices, like giving away a Bible, filled me with bewildered gratitude; they possessed generosity beyond anything I had ever taught them. Other decisions, like leaving a brother behind, filled me with smoldering wrath. How could they be so careless of each other's lives?

My faith in Erik and Mark hung suspended in a chasm of doubt. How would they survive when life and death in the wilderness hinged on a single decision? Had we done enough, over the years, to teach them wisdom in their endeavors? And how would a wilderness education play against a young man's perception of invincibility? I could do little beyond pray to a God who I hoped was more merciful than the unforgiving landscape on which we lived.

On another level, I could not help but think about where we were headed in this tumble of emotion, in a churning free fall away from each other. The realization that we could, without regret, disappoint each other filled me with a sense of both foreboding and longing.

"Where does faith go when it falls?" I wondered. And I watched as white water poured into the hand of the rock.

DEVIL'S PASS

E rik and Mark took up mountain biking when they were thirteen and fifteen years old, respectively. They worked odd jobs, saved their allowances, and bartered cash in exchange for birthday gifts until they had enough money to buy fat, knobby-tired bicycles. They talked about their bikes with the affection of boys in love with cars, comparing shocks, handlebars, brake systems, and tire rims. They pored over catalogs and dreamed about replacing current bike parts with those of vastly superior quality. I asked them once what difference say, a new fork—the two-pronged metal support that holds the front wheel in place—could make in the enjoyment of a ride along a mountain trail. The hum of conversation stopped as they both stared at me in disbelief and pity. I simply didn't understand.

It was true. I didn't understand. More and more, the boys were growing mysterious to me. I wrote it off as teenage bravado and told myself that someday they would come to their senses. I couldn't yet conceive that they might love something beyond my knowing. This is not to say I didn't try to comprehend. I rode from our house to the river one day, hoping to catch the enthusiasm the boys felt for their new-found sport. The boys had found a new trail and Mark invited me to experience the fun—it was the perfect place to introduce me to his new passion. Erik was off on some other venture and I looked forward to spending time with my youngest son.

The first half of our trip rolled along pavement until we reached the woods that sloped toward Eagle River. My bike was a twenty-dollar garage sale special, and although hardly the high-performance bicycles that the boys rode, mine had the thick treaded tires needed to traverse bumpy terrain. We left the pavement and started downhill on a trail that quickly grew rougher with tree roots bulging across the path. As we built up momentum, trees and ferns whizzed past in a jarring blur. With each bump the trail jumped and skipped across my brain like a flickering movie reel. I rode the brakes hard, but still I careened uncontrollably down the hill while trees and rocks rushed at me with ominous animation. I eventually managed to skid to a stop by white-knuckling the brakes and putting my feet on the ground. Mark was too far ahead for me to tell him I'd had enough. This went against every basic tenet of biking I knew—every principle of balance and control. I walked the bike the rest of the way and met Mark at the bottom of the hill. His face was flushed, his eyes wild with enthusiasm.

"Wasn't that great?" he asked. "What took you so long?"

I didn't want to disappoint him, but I admitted that his pace was too fast for me. "I'm not sure my brakes are working very well," I said. "I had a hard time stopping."

"Why would you want to stop?" Mark wondered.

"The bumps on the trail jar my arms and head," I said. "How do you steer down the hill without rattling your teeth?"

Mark looked at my garage-sale bike. Disdain crept into his eyes and he shook his head. "What you need is a new fork with good shocks."

I remained unconvinced. A hiking pace allowed the senses to absorb the sights and sounds of the mountains. I could touch the cool fronds of ferns along the way. Taste the tangy sweetness of ripening berries. Smell the scent of rain.

To me it seemed that speed and the sensation of imminent disaster could spoil a wilderness experience. Bewildered, I left mountain biking to the boys. One weekend they asked me to drive and pick them up from a trail called Devil's Pass. The twenty-eight mile trek started in the foothills of the

Kenai Mountains, a two-hour drive from home. Devil's Pass climbed three thousand feet to Resurrection Pass. From there it descended along valleys and creek beds until it reached another trailhead on the highway, some fifty miles from the drop-off point.

It had been raining all week. The night before, I warned the boys that if the weather didn't let up they would have to reschedule their trip. We woke that morning to a light drizzle. The boys pleaded and I relented on one condition: if we didn't see a few sun breaks by the time we got to the trailhead, we would turn around.

We picked up their friends Jake and Matt on the way out of town. The clouds cooperated and the sun beamed patches of light on the ocean water as we skirted the mountains along the Turnagain Arm of Cook Inlet. The scenic drive and anticipation of the day ahead had all four boys in a buoyant mood. While they told stories and laughed about previous adventures, I interrupted with questions. Did they have extra bicycle tubes to repair flat tires? Had they packed bear repellent? And the cell phone?

When we arrived at the trailhead the boys adjusted their helmets, oiled their chains, and with hardly a backward glance, pedaled onto the muddy trail. It was here at the point of departure that the prayers began. *Keep them safe, Lord. Forgive any lapses of judgment. Keep the bears away. Guard and guide them.*

The plan was to meet six hours later at the pickup point. The boys had not been gone for fifteen minutes when the sky closed again and it began to rain in earnest. I looked at the darkening sky and wished I could will the boys back. I wished I had another cell phone to call them and tell them to try this adventure another day. But their cell phone wasn't on. We had agreed they should leave it turned off to conserve the batteries for an emergency. There was nothing to be done but continue praying.

I wasn't interested in hiking in the downpour so I drove to the nearby coastal community of Seward. The SeaLife Center had recently opened and I decided to see the ocean's wildlife from the dry comfort of a museum-like setting. I tried not to think about the rain pelting against the huge glass windows. Turning away from the gray view overlooking Resurrection Bay, I looked inside the interactive tanks and touched the sea anemones. Their gelatin-like fingers closed reflexively around mine. Then I discovered a sea star that had me gazing into the tank for the better part of an hour. This creature—a basket star—glowed a pure, translucent white. Dozens of branched arms, as delicate as tatted lace, swayed gently in the water. Each arm's tiny tendrils curled and uncurled in graceful motion. I wondered at this marvel of creation—at the Mind behind such an intricate design. Was this the same God of crashing storms, rumbling tectonic plates, and mountain peaks set against an azure sky? It occurred to me that only a Creator who loves with tenderness could have conceived of such a thing as this little white sea star. I pressed my hand against the cool glass, using my fingers to outline its shape.

I left the SeaLife Center and drove to the pickup point early. An hour passed. I tried to read but my eyes drifted off the page and through the sheets of water that rained down the windshield. The patter of rain grew into the insistent drumbeat of a downpour. Another hour passed. Now the kids were officially late—past the window of time we allotted for incidental stops along the way. My mind raced with possibilities as my foot tapped frenetic pace with the sound of rain on the roof. What had happened? I chewed the inside of my mouth until I tasted blood.

Too nervous to sit still any longer, I put on a jacket, tightened the laces of my boots, and headed up the trail. Eventually the rocky trail turned into a torrent of water, deep enough in places to flow over the top of my leather hiking boots. I thought about bicycle tires and brake systems and shock-absorbing handlebar forks. No manufacturer in the world could design a bike for these riding conditions.

A mile into the mountains, a lone bicyclist bumbled toward me. His wheels wobbled as he hit submerged rocks on the trail. He'd just ridden ten miles and no he hadn't seen four teenage boys on the trail that day. Rain dripped from his helmet, his face was spattered with mud, and he looked eager to be on his way. But I stood in the middle of the trail quizzing him further. Was he sure he had seen no sign of the boys? He shook his head firmly and I moved to let him pass.

By now I too was soaked and cold. Maybe the boys had only gotten a few miles into the trip and turned back. Maybe they had called home with a message to pick them up at the original trailhead. I turned back toward the car and drove to a nearby campground to call home. No word or messages from the boys. I called their cell phone. No answer. Fear constricted in my chest like a hot fist. My husband flew professionally for a National Guard search and rescue unit. I called him and explained that the boys were two hours late.

"They'll show up," Todd said. "If not, there's nothing to do until the weather clears."

Nothing to do. That was the worst of it. Only the imagination could fill in the missing blanks of the day.

Bike trouble. One of my qualms with mountain biking is the potential for mechanical problems. Flat tires, derailed chains, broken cables all grind an expedition to a halt. The boys carried spare brake pads and inner tubes. But having to carry a disabled bike to the end of the trail could take all day. Wouldn't two of them ride ahead to let me know about the trouble? Wouldn't someone at least have called home and left a message? Granted, cell phones don't always work in the folds of mountain passes. But couldn't they have called from the higher elevations of the pass? Something had gone terribly wrong.

God preserve them.

Injury. One of the boys may have fallen on the trail and been badly injured. The boys' friend, a tomboy girl, once rode solo on a backcountry trail and fell, breaking her arm. She rode out by herself, one hand on the handlebars, the other dangling painfully at her side. A broken leg would make riding or walking out of Devil's Pass impossible. In the rain and cold, hypothermia and shock would quickly set in. Would the boys recognize the disorientation that comes from dehydration and hypothermia—even without an injury? The boys had emergency foil blankets, extra clothing, and food. Still, what about a broken skull? The guys notoriously left their helmets unbuckled. My only comfort was that there were four of them—surely someone would be coming down the trail for help soon.

God help them.

Bears. We often see bear along hillsides as we hike. We avoid those we see—the ones we don't see are the ones that worry us. Mountain biking seemed a perfect setup for an unexpected bear encounter—speed, the sound of wind and rain drowning out other noises, and myopic concentration on the trail immediately in front of the tire. Bears possess powerful reflexes, claws that can fillet human flesh, and jaws that crush bones. Which boy would be leading the pack? How would the others respond to seeing a friend shaken and torn like a rag doll? Who would ride for help while the others attended to a bleeding buddy?

Come Lord Jesus.

Absurdly, as the wait grew interminable, I pictured their funerals. Funerals for each of them separately. For all of them together. Beside each closed casket stood a table covered with smiling pictures and personal items. Erik and Mark shared a table. Erik's ear-chewed teddy bear rested against a tackle box of trout flies he had tied himself. Mark's worn hiking boots sat among Calvin and Hobbes books and drawings of his original cartoon character, "Shrimp Boy." In the center of the table stood a photo of the boys with their arms draped over each other's shoulders—grinning into the camera after a mud fight. Mourners filed past weeping.

A copper haze of guilt suffused these images. I imagined grief and yet knew in my bones that no amount of imagining would equal the pain of actually losing any one of them. Would I be given these children to nurture and protect only to have them torn from my grasp? Yet children died every day— children whose parents were not accomplices to the fact, who did not allow their children to play in dangerous places.

I supposed that losing what we love was like peeling away layers of attachment until there was nothing left but the hot, tender core of our being, raw and unprotected. From this flows either trust or despair. I did not, at the moment, care to experience either. I just wanted the boys to appear before my eyes. My prayer became a single thought, spoken inwardly over and over. A mantra and a plea.

Please.

Over three hours late, the boys straggled in from the trail, wet, miserable, and covered with mud. They'd had bike trouble, used every spare inner tube on flat tires, and worn their brake pads right into the metal rims of their wheels. The torrential rain had sent them into the shelter of a Forest Service cabin where they had eaten and warmed themselves before continuing on the trail. The waterlogged cell phone didn't work. The video camera they'd used to document their exploits along the way had also stopped working. No one had been hurt. No, they hadn't seen any bears. The rain sucked.

Mark's shoulders shook and his teeth chattered. I insisted they dig out an emergency blanket. Mark pulled it around himself and sat in the front seat with the heater blasting. The other boys loaded the bikes. I could hardly believe my luck to have them all in the vehicle again. Never had the smell of dirty hair, sweaty feet, and mud smelled so sweet. My fevered heart retreated back into my rib cage.

I watched them, looking for signs of serious hypothermia. Beyond the mud, I saw in each of them traces of the little boys I once knew. Erik's blueberry eyes and wheat-colored hair. The smooth lines of Mark's face set against his stormy eyes.

Matt and Jake's daring. The hot coal that had smoldered with fear in the pit of my stomach suddenly burned with intense love for them all. A great rush of wings, like thousands of birds breaking free of gravity's grip, fanned the flame. No rush the boys experienced in their mountain biking adventures could compare with the lurching joy I felt at having them here at this moment. I wanted to gather them into my arms. Cradle their muddy faces in my hands. Sing at the top of my lungs.

As the boys settled into their seats, grim faces broke into smiles. They looked at each other and began to laugh. Erik's spattered face looked like an appaloosa's rear end. Mark resembled a burrito wrapped in foil. Jake's red curls hung in brown stringy strands and mud on Matt's upper lip gave him a perfect Hitler mustache.

They each told their stories, their own version of things. The trail, their falls, the unbelievable amount of rain that had descended. Over the course of the day they had added to their collection a memory none of them would forget—the kind of memory that, strung together with other adventures, create the colorful strands of a full life. Their relief at having finished the trek expanded into an unwavering belief that the whole experience had been great fun. Their only complaint was hunger. They were starving.

We stopped at Gwins, a log-cabin café with a slanted floor and seven small wooden tables. The waitress sized up the four dripping teenagers standing in the doorway, then looked at me.

"We have a lost and found box—your guys are welcome to take anything in it if they want to change into some dry clothes." It was typical wilderness hospitality—take what you need and give when you can. The boys declined the offer for clothes but asked if they could order something to go. They were ready to get home.

A single order for cheeseburger, fries, and a drink cost twelve dollars. I nodded. The price seemed beside the point. "We'll take four."

The boys piled back into the vehicle and attacked their meal with ardor, groaning with pleasure as they ate. Amid the smell of ketchup and the thumping rhythm of windshield wipers, a quiet stillness descended upon me. From the debris of dread emerged a white, translucent tenderness and two fervent words.

Thank you.

Kesugi Ridge

Getting out of the house was the toughest part. I had to arrange care for the dog and cat and the garden. Bills had to be paid; groceries needed to be bought for the trip and for the forlorn family left behind. More than just the logistical aspects of stocking the larder for four days, a certain separation anxiety descended upon the household before I left. I'm not sure if it belonged to me or to the boys, but I told myself that this was good for them. It let them know I was not as indispensable as they might imagine, and that yes, they could manage on their own. They were, after all, old enough to drive.

Erik and Mark planned their own overnight camping trip with friends that weekend. Todd would be out of town and I wondered, "Who will be home to take their call if someone gets hurt?" A sticky film of guilt clung to my preparations.

As much as I'd looked forward to independent travel since our trip to Faith Falls, this first backpacking trip without my sons felt reckless. Like desertion. The only rationale for the outing was my desire to be there, to experience something for no one's sake but my own.

Kesugi Ridge stretches 27.5 miles across the backbone of Denali State Park. The state park sidles up against the larger, better-known Denali National Park roughly in the lower center of the state. The guidebook listed this hike as "strenuous," a challenging traverse with sweeping views of Mt. McKinley and the Alaska Range. The trail ran north and south with a total elevation gain of 5,400 feet.

My friend Gaye organized annual expeditions into the backcountry and after several years of deferring her invitation, I finally accepted. Gaye, a business teacher and accountant, called herself an armchair mountaineer but I considered her the real thing. No other woman I knew seized every opportunity for outdoor adventure. Like me, she was not particularly athletic, yet her drive and enthusiasm carried her dreams for exploring the backcountry.

I knew most of the group—several of us went to the same church.

Lori, a woman with blonde braids and slender hands, worked as an elementary school teacher sporting the cheerful countenance of those who enjoy their work with children.

Christy, also a teacher, drew often from a deep well of encouragement that resided in her bones, and this she shared freely with all of us. Fair-haired and gently freckled, her green backpack dwarfed her diminutive frame.

Teri's broad smile and optimism showcased her profession as a dentist. She wore a yellow bandanna around her neck. I knew from other hikes with her that she would take the bandanna off at stream crossings, dip it into the icy water and used it as a washcloth. Rolled up, it also made a handy headband for a sweating brow.

As we stood in the parking lot at the trailhead, Gaye also introduced us to her friends from Fairbanks, Betsy and Tom. They comprised the only couple in the group, and Tom the only man. We teased him about being our token male. Finally, Gaye introduced Sandra from Trapper Creek.

Gaye told me about Sandra before the trip, and I eyed her now with respect and wonder. Short and solid, she smiled broadly without a hint of the past year's tragedy. Her twenty-three-year-old son had died in a car accident just nine months ago. Matt guided mountain climbers on McKinley, a dangerous profession that he loved. A car wreck on a deserted highway in Canada was not how anyone expected him to die. Shortly after his death, the news of breast cancer assaulted Sandra's already ravaged life. This backpacking trip on Kesugi Ridge was her first recreational undertaking since Matt's death, since her radical surgery and aggressive chemotherapy.

How can she walk, stand, even breathe in the vortex of such loss, I wondered? Maybe over the course of the coming days I would learn what reserves she drew on to put one foot in front of the other.

We started down the trail early in the afternoon, at the height of the sun's elliptical journey along the northern sky. This time of year in June, the sun dipped briefly below the horizon at night before rising again. It never grew dark; only a cool twilight cloaked the early morning hours after midnight. Gaye and Sandra took up the rear while Teri and Lori led the pack. Teri's charge left the rest of us stretched out at times over a quarter mile of trail. Christy's ill-fitting backpack threatened to topple her at every turn in the trail. Moss, Sandra's Border collie, toted a red backpack with dog food. He loped along with the leaders of the group, occasionally backtracking to the end of the line to check on Sandra.

The first three miles of the trail climbed gradually uphill. Dwarf dogwood, and wild geraniums bloomed at our feet. A raspberry scent of wild roses sweetened the air. The sun warmed our skin but a cool breeze kept mosquitoes at bay. Above tree line, we hiked the alpine tundra, through a boulder field, and across a rocky gorge to our first night's camping spot. It took almost four hours to traverse five miles.

Sandra and Gaye prepared our first night's meal, a flavorsome medley of fajitas, spicy beans and cheese wrapped in soft tortilla shells. Sitting around the camp kitchen —placed fifty yards from the tents in case bears decided to investigate during the night —we ate enthusiastically. Moss waited politely for us to finish our meal and then cleaned the crumbs off the tundra. Sandra and I talked about dogs and I compared Moss to my gluttonous Labrador. We laughed but did not speak beyond the politeness of strangers. I noticed that the cup she drank from was marked with the name "Matt."

The breeze diminished in the evening hours and the mosquitoes ascended from the tundra in frenzied swarms. How could I forget to bring a head net? I doused myself with bug spray but still breathed mosquitoes into my mouth and nostrils. Finally, when the whine of mosquitoes grew oppressive, Teri and I crawled into our tent. Camping on the slope of a mountain without a level area, we were forced to pitch our tent at an angle with our feet pointing downhill. I left my journal in my backpack at the camp kitchen but wasn't motivated enough to get dressed again and fight the mosquitoes to get it. Throughout the night as we slept, gravity gradually pulled us to the foot of the tent before we scooched back up again. I slept restlessly, as though engaged in battle to free myself from the pull of maternal and domestic concerns. I hoped the boys were safe as they camped tonight on a different and distant hillside.

We woke to clear skies and a stunning view of Mount McKinley. Even on sunny days the 20,320-foot peak is often shrouded in clouds. The mountain is so tall that it creates its own weather. The height of the range catches the moisture-laden air blowing in from the Gulf of Alaska. Snow accumulates year-round, feeding dozens of glaciers, the longest of which snakes forty-six miles through the creases of the mountain's foothills. The Alaska Range separates Alaska's Interior from the more temperate coastal region of Southcentral Alaska.

Locals call the mountain "Denali." According to legend, the mountain formed as a result of a battle between Yako, a brave Indian and the Raven War Chief, Totson. Totson tried to kill Yako by brewing a storm to swamp his canoe. The waves grew higher and higher. When Totson heaved his war spear, Yako deflected it by turning the waves to stone. Totson's canoe crashed into what was now the mountain, throwing him onto the rocks where he changed into a raven. Yako then fell asleep. When he awoke, he named the mountains he created "Denali, the high one," and "Sultana, his wife" (Mt. Foraker).

This morning the white citadel stood before us like some magnificent kingdom. The path of Eldridge Glacier wound through the mountain's foothills. Miles of glacial moraine stretched like striped taffy, white and gray, up the mountainside. Teri and I dug out our cameras and took more pictures than necessary, especially since no 4x6 print would capture the immensity, the raw power of the mountain.

It took the morning to establish a routine of getting breakfast, filtering water for our bottles, and breaking camp. We got a slow start. Tom emerged from his tent and yawned.

"Well, ladies," he said stretching. "Now that I've slept with you I'm afraid we can no longer be friends."

Gaye hooted and volleyed back a disparaging remark which made Tom's wife Betsy laugh. Just outside of ear-shot, I swatted mosquitoes and waited for the water to boil at the camp kitchen. One's addictions become magnified on the trail. I tied my hair into a pony tail and tucked it under my cap. Trying to ease the ache from my throbbing head, I stretched. Lori wondered if I was into yoga.

"No," I said. "I just need a cup of coffee."

After a dose of caffeine and ibuprophen, I ate oatmeal sprinkled with pecans, brown sugar, and raisins.

Finally underway, we felt the sun beat down and gladly absorbed its rays. We knew how quickly the weather could change to deliver slanting rain, frigid wind, or fog. My pack weighed forty pounds. It carried my portion of the tent, a camp stove, food, a water filter, my sleeping bag, and rain gear. It also held a cooking pot, a sleeping mat, bug spray, sunscreen, and a camera. The final three pounds were my revolver and bullets. I wasn't eager to take the gun, but the group consensus was to bring it along in case a bear gave us trouble. I carried the .41 in the top pocket of my pack for easy access.

The trail wound up and down, and we stopped every few hours to peel our packs from our backs and crunch on granola bars and trail mix. I ate big gobs of peanut butter with homemade currant jelly on a thick, round saltine-like cracker called pilot bread. A gourmet meal from a fine restaurant never tasted so good.

The Kesugi Ridge trail extends along the western ridge of the Talkeetna Range, to the east, across a broad valley from the Alaska Range. Angular rock formations rose like stark fortresses against the blue sky. The high point of the trail at 3,500 feet, Stonehenge Hill overlooked the eastern slope of the ridge. The dryer, wind-scoured parts of the trail resembled a moonscape. In contrast, rain-catching valleys grew green and lush with life. Spring wildflowers carpeted the alpine tundra. Deep purple violets, yellow buttercups, and fuchsia-colored moss campion peeked from white beds of lichen.

The last half-mile of the day's trail descended—into a green meadow. The sun that warmed us in the morning grew harsh and unrelenting over the course of the day. The heat began to exhaust some of the hikers. Gaye, in particular, felt feverish. Blisters had bubbled up on Christy's heels. I began to take off my boots and socks during our breaks to relieve hotspots. My feet were soggy, not from rain or river crossings, but from sweat. Sandra held her own, but fatigue lined her face. We sat in the middle of the meadow to rest before finding a final campsite. Gaye looked up and pointed out two dark cloud systems, one on either side of the ridge, moving on a collision course toward us.

"We better get the tents set up. Right now," Gaye said.

Always optimistic, Teri didn't think it would rain, but shrugged and got up as the group moved to set up camp. We climbed as fast as our tired feet would take us to higher ground on the other side of the valley. I offered to set up the tent while Teri quickly made dinner. It was our night to feed the group. Thunder rumbled as we ate a meal of quick rice and Cajun sausage. We didn't have time to savor it; by the time we tucked our dishes away and covered our packs, the sky had grown bruised and yellow. With a flash of lightning, enormous raindrops began pelting our tents and we fled inside, zipping the tent tight against the coming tempest.

What seemed like a sheltered ridge became a funnel for wind and a barrel to hold the brunt of the storm. Lighting split the sky as thunder instantaneously shook the ground. The wind clawed from all directions, bowing our tent poles in and out. Hail began to pound against the tent. Teri and I grinned at each other and started whooping and laughing at every earth-shaking thunderclap.

"Someone needs to invent a transparent tent so we can watch the weather outside," I shouted.

Sounds of yelling from the tent next door filtered through the din of the storm. We assumed that the rest of the group was enjoying nature's performance as much as we were. I risked a spray of rain to peek outside.

With wind whipping her tiny frame, Christy clutched their tent's rain fly that billowed in the wind like a flag. Tom and Betsy scrambled out of their tents to help. Lori attempted to stuff her things into a bag before they grew soaked, an effort that proved futile. Teri insisted there were enough wet people in the group; there was no point in us going out. The next time I looked, Lori stood outside the tent. Without her weight to hold it down, the stakes had pulled out of the soft tundra and the tent lay gasping on its side, like a living, wheezing creature. Slowly the winds began to diminish, the thunder faded, and Christy crawled into the vestibule of our tent.

"We have a major problem," she said breathless, her eyes brimming with tears. "Lori wants to walk out tonight. My feet just can't take anymore today. I've tried to convince her to stay until morning, but she's determined to leave."

Lori, in the other tent, talked to Gaye and Sandra. This was the only place on the 27 ½ mile trail where walking out was even an option. Near the intersection of Ermine Trail, a road lay only five miles to the west. Without Ermine Trail, traveling either north or south required a two-day walk back to civilization.

Christy retreated to Tom and Betsy's tent, wet and shivering. She worried Lori was angry since it was her tent that failed. Although Gaye and Sandra's tent had not blown away, the fabric did not hold up against the battering rain. Only two of the four tents had performed adequately under the assault of the storm. The trail for tomorrow involved a steep descent into a marshy valley followed by a grueling uphill climb to the next camp. Gaye still felt feverish and Sandra was more exhausted than she anticipated. With sleeping bags dripping from the driving rain, it made sense for some of the group to head home. Gaye and Sandra volunteered to hike out with Lori.

Although Christy somehow felt responsible for the evening's disaster, I talked her into staying. She could bunk with Teri and me. Betsy and Tom offered a place in their larger tent as well.

As we loaded the wet gear into Lori, Gaye, and Sandra's backpacks, Christy, who stopped shivering only after warming herself in a sleeping bag, offered turtle chocolates to the hikers for energy on the trail. She was eager to make amends. Gaye offered to take back anything no longer needed for the trail, wet gear, garbage, anything. She felt bad about leaving an expedition that she organized. Everyone, it seemed, wanted to share in the guilt. Lori, wet and bedraggled, squared her shoulders as she stuffed into her backpack the very tent that had spoiled her trip. Even so, no amount of soggy weight was going to deter her from reaching the road that night.

They headed out at 10 p.m. with Alaska's midnight sun filtering through the dissipating clouds. I regretted losing three women (and the dog) of our party. As Sandra's backpack disappeared into the brush, I thought about the missed opportunity to become better acquainted. Why hadn't I stayed behind to talk with her as we hiked? Now I regretted the camp-side discussion Sandra and I would never have.

Gaye later told us they reached the road after midnight. It took nearly an hour before anyone stopped for three soggy backpackers and a wet dog. Gaye's wet pack with the extra gear weighed a staggering fifty-five pounds. What began as a fever the day of the hike developed into a full-blown flu in the days that followed.

In the mean time, Christy climbed into our tent and we began to giggle. Fatigue or maybe the letdown of adrenaline fed our silliness, but we grew giddy as we recounted the evening. What a sight, that overturned tent. And poor Lori, whose dripping braids and grim mouth were the only outward signs of what was likely an inner fury. Who wouldn't be mad? Moss, in terror at the storm, had crawled headfirst into Sandra's sleeping bag with her. Even as we wiped tears of hilarity from our eyes, we hoped there were no hard feelings. We'd all have a good laugh about it again back home.

As we finally drifted off to sleep, I thought about Erik and Mark and how often I had raptly listened to their exploits around the dinner table, admonishing them for their scrapes and close calls. I looked forward to telling them about this storm. And I thought about Sandra, who drank from a cup that once belonged to her son.

The next morning we woke to cloudless skies and a continued view of McKinley. One reason this mountain is so striking is that its vertical relief is over 18,000 feet, greater even than that of Mount Everest. The Alaska Range formed as a result of movement along the Denali Fault, a line that stretches 1,300 miles from the Yukon border down to the Aleutian peninsula. Tectonic activity still triggers volcanoes and earthquakes along what's known as the Pacific ring of fire. Tremors occur frequently in the park and preserve.

We doctored Christy's blisters, and showed her how to use moleskin to relieve the pressure on her heels. Cutting a hole for the blister, we created a moleskin moat around the blister so that her shoes would rub on the soft fabric rather than her feet. Backpacking always reminded me of the importance of our dear feet—how deserving they are of care. The slightest neglect on a trip like this made the experience miserable. In the heat our feet sweat profusely. Wet skin is soft skin, making it more susceptible to soreness. I too had blisters that had formed on the downhill trek to our campsite the day before.

The trail traversed severe ups and downs through heavy brush and mosquito-infested marshes. With temperatures tipping toward the 80s, the deep, undulating valley we crossed became a grueling march. Conversation lapsed to silence as we reached inward for the reserves to continue forward. Moving ahead required a focus that left no room for the frenzied, fragmented distractions of daily life. Thoughts slowed to match the pace of my beating heart, the rhythm of my steps.

The challenging terrain reminded me that shadows and valleys have their home among the mountain peaks. "Yea though I walk through the valley of the shadow of death. . . ." I inwardly spoke the Twenty-third Psalm—the King James Version I'd memorized as a girl—to the tempo and march of my footsteps. I felt the ache in my feet, the weight of my pack, and the burn of sun on my face. And I felt acutely alive. A little like the journey of parenthood, once begun there was no turning back from this—we would reach the end of the trail only by moving forward one step at a time.

This particular expedition was one we chose freely, knowing with relative certainty its outcome. Sometimes life thrusts us upon journeys we would rather not travel, with shadows darker and valleys more painful than we think we are capable of traveling. I supposed that Sandra was traveling that trail already and she lived her life now, one step, and one day at a time. What other choice was there?

And I could not help but remember Mark's accident, the funeral I did not have to attend, and the occasional, still-lingering terror of that possibility. I thought about separation, about how permanent it can become.

My son's accident had left me with deep questions. Whenever I heard of a child dying or read an obituary of a young person's death, I wondered why Mark was spared. Every time we reached a milestone in Mark's life—his confirmation, his first day at junior high, his first driving lesson—I was struck that we could just as easily be commemorating this day at his graveside. Other mothers, like Sandra, came home from the trauma of an accident to an empty room, a room in which only memories remained. She fingered the still toys, his backpack or favorite things. She buried her face in her child's clothes and breathed deeply for the last traces of his scent. How was it that I daily went into Mark's room, ran my fingers through his hair in the morning and said, "Hey sleepyhead. Time to get up for school"?

It was an odd thing, I suppose, in light of the fact that my son survived, to ask God, "Why me?"

Great slabs of rock made up much of the upper trail. While the younger Alaska Range is marked by sheer walls and jagged spires of coal-black flysch and schist, Kesugi Ridge, in the Talkeetna Range, had rolling rock formations that were more rounded, where thick underlying folds of magma cooled into gray granite. Without a defined path, cairns along the way marked the route. Like miniature pagodas or oriental lanterns, several of them were perched on boulders so huge only climbers with technical gear—ropes and ascenders—could have reached the top to place them there.

It occurred to me as we hiked how attached we humans are to the props of our lives. Here we were trekking along with everything we needed placed neatly on our backs. When the weight of it became burdensome, each of us mentally considered what we might leave behind next time.

For example, I normally don't bring camp shoes or sandals when I'm backpacking; but most other hikers are willing to carry the weight of an extra pair of shoes in order to enjoy that comfort at the end of the day. Compare this decision (one pair of shoes or two?) with the closets full of shoes and boots in any given household and it becomes apparent that what we consider the "necessities" of life are really only comforts and conveniences.

As I hiked, I thought about my cupboards full of pots and pans and dishes, the countertops littered with appliances, the cars in my driveway. I considered how the weight of it all could consume us; how little by little, our souls grew cramped under the load of our growing possessions. It seemed a travesty that I'd ever allowed a day to go by that I didn't go outdoors, breathe deeply of fresh air and examine, however briefly, some aspect of creation. A spider's web. A blade of grass. An ice crystal.

When we finally decided on our camping spot, we all dropped our packs on the ground, kicked off our boots, and lay on the tundra without speaking. The heat and a breeze kept the mosquitoes away and we lay there until I felt my skin burning under the blaze of sun. By this, the third evening and without a storm to contend with, the shyness of strangers had evolved into an easy camaraderie. We laughed at each other as we got up again to set up camp. We moved with geriatric steps, hobbling and hunched over on tender feet.

It was so very pleasant not to deal with mosquitoes this evening. We sat around our camp stove as chicken and rice and vegetables simmered in the pot. We swapped stories about other trails and adventures we'd undertaken, and when we finally dished the steaming food onto our plates the meal had become a kind of communion.

"Hey look," Betsy said. "There's a bear over on that far ridge."

In the golden light of evening, a black bear loped across the rolling hillside. Teri dug out her binoculars and we passed them around to get a closer look. The bear stopped awhile, snuffled around an outcropping of brush, and then galloped over the side of the ridge. We marveled at our good fortune. It never even occurred to us to reach for the gun.

When we got into our tents, we seemed to radiate back all the heat our skin had absorbed over the long day. It was difficult to sleep, and yet I, for one, was tired beyond reason. We'd hiked nine miles, but it felt more like twenty. The plan was to sleep in and hike out to the end of the trail at a leisurely pace the next morning. We had only five miles to go, much of it a steep downhill.

We woke to the rumble of thunder at 5:30 a.m. and decided to get on the trail before another storm hit. My feet protested as I tried to fit them into my boots. It seemed the boots had shrunk overnight, or my feet had grown two sizes. The mosquitoes that stayed hidden in yesterday's heat assaulted us with ravenous frenzy. I took a picture of Teri attempting to eat breakfast with her cup and spoon tucked inside the head net on her head. I spat mosquitoes out of my mouth and swore never again to forget a head net.

Every rock and turn in the trail seemed to bruise the bones of my feet. I wrested my attention from my feet and focused on the view before us. The storm passed without event and the combination of morning sun against the dark storm clouds deepened the light around the mountains. Square angular rocks the size of houses littered the hillside like a cemetery for giants.

The heady scent of the wildflowers, ferns, and dense foliage greeted us as we descended below the timberline toward the end of the trail. While the others seemed eager to get back, I fought back feelings of melancholy. Already my mind wandered ahead toward home and I wondered what I might face on the domestic front. Had the boys stayed out of trouble? Been safe? Would Todd be in good spirits when I returned? A pensive look from any one of them could sabotage my joy. Accuse me of neglect. The more I thought about it, the more a reluctant weight settled on my chest. The apprehension of leave-taking four days ago had become something else altogether. Expansive views, newfound friends, the challenges of the trail create new spaces in the architecture of the spirit. And I wondered how to wedge myself back into the established forms I myself had created.

As Hours Will

I stood at the darkened door of my fifteen-year-old son's bedroom, watching the even rise and fall of his breathing. An hour ago we were locked in battle, harsh words followed by hot tears. He lay in his bed as we argued, his head propped on a man-sized hand. The muscles of his shoulders bulged in his nearly six-foot frame. His eyebrows formed a solid, angry line across his brow. At times the veins in his neck swelled as he strained to control his emotions.

An image came to mind as I watched this man-child, so serene now in sleep. It was a poster I saw once, a close-up picture of legs wearing jeans torn and worn out at the knees. Across the poster, printed in bold letters, were the words "Pray Hard." As a parent, I felt like my jeans were not just worn—my knees were bloody, stripped to bone and sinew. I didn't know if God listened more carefully or was more apt to answer prayers that came so earnestly en masse. But I found myself on my knees a lot, my only refuge in the stormy landscape of my sons' adolescence.

Mark, fifteen, and Erik, nearly seventeen, were decent people—good workers, average students, and civic-minded young men. When they managed, in their hormonal turbulence, to see past themselves for a moment, I saw in them the makings of compassionate, caring young men.

Erik, a peacemaker, was born wiser than his years. As an infant, he stared past me with a smile of such recognition and gentle joy that it startled me; I would spin around to see who stood behind us. Erik seemed to see things I couldn't, and I wondered for the first time about the presence of angels. Todd claimed Erik was an unnaturally happy kid. I thought of him as supernaturally happy—since age ten he had wanted to be a minister. He was also extraordinarily absentminded, a chronic procrastinator and messy beyond belief. He once hatched flies in his room because of a forgotten biology experiment. More than once, we took away his driving privileges until he cleaned and fumigated the car. Athletic gear and the remains of rotting lunches created such a stench I had to drive with the windows open.

Mark carried a fiery torch of intensity. Sometimes the flame burned with exhilaration. Other times it burned with fury. There wasn't much in-between for this kid. He had a brilliant, at times acerbic, wit and was driven by laughter and adventure. He lived on the edge, pressing his abilities at extreme sports like backcountry skiing, biking, and mountain climbing. The closer he came to disaster without it actually befalling him, the better. Yes, this was the child whose bleeding, crumpled body I once held after he was struck by a car as an eight year old. Often angry—Mark could not tolerate injustice, yet he perceived it all around him. If he ever found a crusade to call his own, he would be a force to be reckoned with. In the meantime he battled the tyranny of authority in general—teachers, parents, his orthodontist (the Incompetent Idiot).

My prayers for the boys took several directions. One was simply for physical safety. While we used to hike, backpack, and ski together—their expeditions now left me far behind in both expertise and endurance. So I prayed that God would watch over them and compensate for any lack of judgment. The boys believed wholeheartedly in their invincibility. I knew better and I prayed that the realization of their mortality would not cost them (or me) too much.

Another prayer for them was for spiritual safety. I prayed that they would not be warped by a world that demands the worship of wealth and beauty and power. I prayed that they would listen to the gentle voices that speak to them from within and without. "Let them always hear Your voice," I prayed. "And let them never forget the voices of the poor or the oppressed."

And then there was another realm of prayer, often wordless, usually exasperated. This silent supplication had to do with the boys growing into men. Emily Dickinson wrote:

> *The Hours slid fast—as Hours will,*
> *Clutched tight, by greedy hands*
> *So faces on two Decks, look back,*
> *Bound to opposing lands.*

Greedily I clutched at the time left before the boys disappeared into manhood—an island that, by gender, I would never enter nor ever fully understand.

Disillusion hit especially hard during a discussion with Erik that began at dinner and ended late into the night. We were clearing dishes together. Mark had disappeared into his room to do homework. Todd sat in the living room watching the evening news. Amidst the scrape and clank of dishes, Erik announced that he felt women did not belong in the military. He insisted that women should not serve in combat roles because it would distract men, who would feel compelled to rescue them. This, of course, would compromise the mission.

I bristled and asked, "Why should women, who are qualified, be denied the opportunity to serve in any capacity just because of someone's ego problem?"

Erik went on to discuss the role of men and women using Biblical examples to support his point of view. I felt the color rising in my neck. The task at hand grew noisier as I placed dishes into the dishwasher with energetic force. Where had he learned such nonsense? Not from me. Politically I called myself a moderate. Since my more conservative husband was so often away from home, I always assumed the boys would take after mom in their philosophical leanings. Instead, Erik was in shocking agreement with the traditional church's patriarchal hierarchy.

"You must take into consideration the cultural context in which the Bible was written," I stormed at him. "Surely you don't believe that God condones the culture of slavery or the denigration of women. God simply used that particular historical context because it was the one available at the time."

We went around and around—Erik, the peacemaker, and me, the pacifist and quasi-feminist, unusually and powerfully at odds. "Christ teaches freedom!" I rallied. "God teaches submission," Erik protested. "Yes," I countered, "but submission only to God!"

Erik was amused at my fury. "Gosh, Mom," he said, "I didn't know you were such a feminist."

At this point in our conversation, Todd walked in smirking with self-satisfaction. I could just hear him thinking, "Sic 'em, boy." This infuriated me further. I used to joke that I was married to a chauvinist and was raising two little piglets. As it turned out, the last laugh was on me.

"If your name was Erika," I said, "I would fight to the bitter end to see that you were afforded all the opportunities that your brother and father enjoy."

"Aw, come on," he said. "There are lots of things guys aren't allowed to do that only women can do."

"Aside from childbirth, name one!" I challenged him.

He thought awhile. "Well," he said, "guys don't go to baby showers."

I looked at him. He looked at me. The intensity of the conversation coupled with the absurdity of his remark suddenly struck us as comical. We both burst out laughing.

Erik eventually went to bed, no hard feelings. He was nothing, if not agreeable, even when we harbored opposing views. But I stayed up, amazed and troubled. Who was this boy? And what kind of man was he growing up to be? I prayed a lot that night, that God would guide Erik in all the places where I had obviously failed him. (I've heard it said that you can safely assume you've created God in your own image when He agrees with all your political views.)

I also grieved. It grew clearer each day that the boys were moving irretrievably away from me. And while this was not a bad thing—little boys are meant to grow up—I was devastated at how much it felt like abandonment. For weeks afterward, as I watched my family of men share a hearty machismo around the dinner table, I felt utterly alone.

This loneliness sent me into a dark corner of mordancy. I began to wonder. What was the point of this parenting exercise? If it meant nothing to these guys—if all I held dear was lost on them—what was the use of all those sleepless nights, of agonizing choices, of pouring myself into the role of nurse, cook, disciplinarian, advisor, and even, friend? I'd spent, to date, nearly half my life nurturing these kids to adulthood and suddenly the whole enterprise felt like a waste. The past felt like a windblown desert. What had become of all this toil and worry and heartfelt prayer of mine? I had the sinking sense it all would have turned out the same without me.

Not long after my heated discussion with Erik, we entered the season of Lent, a time to reflect on Christ's passion. It began with Ash Wednesday when Erik and Mark and I, along with the rest of the congregation, knelt at the altar. As always, our pastor marked a cross on our foreheads and said, "From ashes you have come; to ashes you will return." After the evening service we went to the store for milk, and realized people were staring at us. We looked at each other and realized that the crosses the pastor had painted were huge and dark, with little crumbles of charcoal still clinging to our skin. Erik's forehead looked like a target. We chuckled. Our pastor was young and enthusiastic.

By the time we got home and started getting ready for bed, our laughter was replaced by slamming doors and sour looks. We'd just returned from a sacrament in which mortality was made very clear, yet we were unable to set aside conflict for a single evening. I don't even remember what the argument was about. I just remember the feeling that the target was painted on my heart.

I crawled into bed but sleep was a long time coming. The question, "What is the point?" kept pressing against my thoughts. I watched the pale green numbers of the alarm clock tick past the minutes. Eventually I got up, pulled the curtain aside and looked out the window. A full moon cast shadows on the snow. Maybe it was a stretch to think of raising teenagers as a personal persecution. But at times their growing up felt like betrayal. The loose ends of emotion seemed to tatter in the hot winds of futility. I realized this was my problem, not the boys'. They were just kids, trying to find their way, unsure of boundaries, the world, and themselves.

My recent argument with Mark had been over his tone of voice. He had raised his voice to me, shouted at me for startling him. It was all quite silly. As I'd walked through the hallway, I'd noticed the dog lying on the forbidden living room carpet. I issued a sharp command just as I passed by the bathroom, where Mark, in deep concentration, was inspecting his face in the mirror. He jumped and yelled, "Mom, what do you think you're doing? Knock it off!"

"Never, under any circumstances, will you yell at your mother!" I shouted back.

He accused me of being on a power trip, of exacting a double standard. He was, to a degree, right on both counts. But I did not back down. "I am willing to entertain any discussion about any matter," I said. "But I will not entertain disrespect."

"How can you demand respect when you don't give it," Mark bellowed, his eyes filling with tears. "You won't even listen to reason. Besides, respect has to be *earned*."

I wanted to slap him. Shove him against the wall. Our argument disintegrated into further accusations until trembling, knowing I teetered on the edge of violence, I said, "This conversation is over."

"Good," Mark said, flopping over so his back faced me. "I need some sleep."

Proverbs says not to let the sun set on your anger. This was not an option for me, since I could not sleep when conflict rocked our household. In the dark quiet of the night, anger dissolved into sadness. I clicked on my bed light, rested a book on my lap as a makeshift desk, and reached for a piece of paper. I could not help myself—I spent an hour writing Mark a letter. I chose my words carefully this time, reiterating my expectation of respectful behavior. But I went on to write how much I admired him—his courage, his sense of humor, his intelligence. I told him that he was more important to me than he could imagine. I folded the piece of paper and stood in the doorway to his room.

Maybe this sleepless night was a waste. Maybe these words to him were just more hot wind across a dry desert. I set the letter on his desk and then bent over him. I wanted to press my lips to his warm cheek, breathe in the scent of his curly hair. But I did not want to wake him, could not bear that he might turn his back on me. And in the end, I kept a tender distance.

GHOST BEAR

I went looking for bears and I knew where to find them. One of several trails radiating from a nature center ten miles from my house had recently closed because of bears feeding on the late run of red salmon in Eagle River. Surprise encounters along the heavily wooded trail in years past had ended unhappily for both people and bears. The route along the river bottom was cordoned off with yellow tape like the scene of a crime. But the upper trails remained open and I headed for the beaver pond. The area was fairly open with a good view of the surrounding mountains. The water below the beaver dam teemed with salmon. Signs posted along the trails warned that a brown bear had been seen feeding in the area earlier in the week.

I went unarmed while back home my house looked like a war zone. Ammunition was stacked on the kitchen counters;

camouflage clothing littered the living room floor. Open gun cases gaped like hungry mouths waiting for the variety of weapons that would accompany my two sons, my husband, a brother-in-law, and two friends into the Alaska bush. They spent months planning this annual harvest and would spend the rest of their lives remembering it. Stories of their exploits in the wilderness grew legendary around the campfire and the kitchen table. Like those of warriors home from the battlefield, their stories formed epic tales of grand adventures.

I could not, however, comprehend their quest. Perhaps they possessed some primal desire to wrestle with the wild and come out victorious. They found satisfaction in providing meat for the tribe and from taking sustenance from the land. From a gardener's perspective, I supposed I understood this. But I was an outsider to their delight of conquest, and the lens through which I attempted to understand was veiled by sensibilities as mysterious to them as their hunt was to me.

This year, along with moose and caribou, animals that provided meat for our family year-round, the guys would be hunting for brown bear. Their special subsistence permits allowed them to hunt for the meat, but not the trophy value of the bear. If they killed a brown bear, they would not be allowed to keep the claws or head. They could keep the hide and were required to pack out the meat. Although they would honor the law, I knew the guys didn't care about the meat. They just wanted to match their hunting skills against a predator of intelligence and prowess and mythological strength.

Maybe I went looking for bears out of protest.

Our sons, Erik and Mark, had grown tall and muscular, and were crack shots with a rifle. Their interest in the outdoors now included my husband Todd's love for hunting and fishing. As I watched them prepare for their adventure, joking with each other about who was the better shot, I remembered sitting around a campfire when they were youngsters. Mark had a jack-o'-lantern grin, his mouth full of gaps and adult teeth too big for his little-boy face. Erik, serious and contemplative, sat leaning against me with easy affection as we roasted hotdogs over the flames. That moment, with the scent of wood smoke in the air and with the whispered song of a creek in the background, I felt utterly, unalterably connected to these boys. They were my homeland, the port at which all good and meaningful things were anchored.

Their joy for this fall's hunt was now so outside my grasp, so beyond my sharing, that they had begun to seem like a foreign land to me. The boys I thought I knew so well were disappearing into a territory that seemed to me shadowy and uncertain.

Mark, seventeen, sported a wild mop of brown hair and intense, brooding eyes. He claimed that hunting moose and caribou no longer posed much of a challenge. Given the opportunity, animals of prey run away. But a bear. Now that was different. A bear was a predator and could kill a man with the swipe of a paw. Mark would have preferred to use a bow and arrow rather than the 30.06 that he was assigned for the hunt. Part of me admired him for wanting to even the odds— as long as someone backed him up with a big bore rifle. A larger part of me wanted Mark to put the animal in his sites and then lower the gun and let the bear eat berries in peace.

Erik, nineteen, was more philosophical and ambivalent about the prospect of killing a bear. His blue eyes narrowed as he thought about the upcoming hunt. "A bear is at the apex of Alaska's ecosystem," he said. "It seems to me that on the evolutionary scale, all other species of animals and plants are lesser beings. If there is a moral dilemma about hunting for bear, it would be the act of taking the best thing that nature has to offer."

I wondered what he would do when he put his sites on brown fur shimmering in the evening sun. Of course he would have his brother, his dad, and the other hunters to answer to—guys whose second favorite pastime after hunting was the sport of ridicule.

Todd sees bears as direct competitors for the moose and caribou that he himself wants to harvest. He hunts bears out of a conviction that wildlife mismanagement and the lack of predator control have created an ecological imbalance, diminishing the supply of game meat. He will shoot a bear to save moose and caribou from losing their calves to an over-abundance of predators. Bears account for about seventy percent of moose calf mortality. If moose and caribou have the opportunity to grow up, they will produce more calves and thus more game to hunt.

My feelings about bears are a mix of awe and wary respect. Bears are beautiful, graceful animals whose fierce-ness in defense of their cubs I admire. Their presence in the mountains and backcountry and in Eagle River Valley where I live remind me that humans are not the all-powerful creatures that we like to imagine. I am not naive. I know that bears pose a potentially lethal risk to people—including my own family and friends.

And yet, the endless hours of preparation for the hunt—the boxes of shotgun shells and rifle bullets, the mounds of tents and sleeping bags, the ropes and tarps and other accou-trements all seem excessive to me.

It annoys me the way taxidermists pose mounted bears. Invariably the bear stands on hind legs, with lips curled to reveal fearsome teeth, and with claws extended. As a matter of fact, bears stand on their hind legs when they are curious and want a better look at something. The stance is not one of aggression. The bear was most likely shot as it grazed a long a sunny hillside, not as it tried to attack the hunter. But suppose the bear did rise up on hind legs before charging. Unless it is hunting season and you are licensed to kill a bear, state law requires that anyone shooting a bear in defense of life or property must skin the animal and relinquish the hide, head, and claws to fish and game authorities. The hides are then tanned and sold at auction. And supposing that someone could legally keep the cape of an attack bear, I find it hard to imagine that anyone would want the reminder of a terrifying bear encounter posed in the corner of the family den. Most snarling mounts of bears are fabrications; poses that imply that the bear was aggressive and that the hunter was brave.

Bears, universal characters in many Native American stories, represent qualities of power, healing, and gentle strength. The Tlingit people say that the bear Kasha is the Great Mother that gave birth to all animals. Because of their humanlike qualities, bears were believed by many West Coast Natives to be Elder Kinsmen. When killed, the hide of the bear was taken to the chief and treated as a high-ranking guest.

A Native Gwich'in woman once told me about a family of bears she and her brother encountered one spring when she was in her early twenties. Velma Wallis, author of *Two Old Women*, *Bird Girl*, and *Raising Ourselves*, is a short, cherub-shaped woman with high, arching cheekbones and a small nose. Her eyes crinkle into curved slivered moons when she smiles. But as she told this story, she was not smiling, not even twenty years later.

Her older brother had been drinking, and as their flat-bottomed boat roared around a corner of the river near their home on the Yukon River, they startled a mother black bear and her two cubs. The cubs scampered up a tree and the mother disappeared into the brush. Her brother idled the engine and grabbed his rifle.

"Don't shoot the cubs," Velma protested. He ignored her, took aim and squeezed off a shot. Velma screamed as one of the cubs crumpled and fell from the tree. Her brother laughed at her.

"What I didn't know at the time," Velma said, her voice growing quiet, "is that I was pregnant." Tears welled in her eyes. "Not long after this happened, I miscarried."

She paused and looked at the napkin she had folded, and unfolded it again. "I know it sounds crazy, but I'm convinced that mother bear took away my baby, just like my brother took away hers."

The first time I went looking for the bear, I brought our dog, Sue, and watched from the trail. I looked for the closest tree I might climb and calculated how long it would take to climb it. I mentally measured the distance between the dam and the trail where I was standing—maybe fifty yards. Staying on the trail, I stood behind tall stalks of cow parsnip so that I was not so obviously in view should a bear arrive on the scene.

Sue grew confused at my stillness. She was used to rigorous, extended hikes. So far we'd only traveled a short mile. She trotted to the water, drank, and came back to stand beside me. With mild interest, she watched as two beavers played in the pond, pushing folds of glassy water as they swam. Although she was an agreeable companion, with an uncanny sense to leave wildlife alone on our excursions, she distracted me, drawing me into a familiar state of maternal concern. I could climb a tree, but she couldn't. Besides, no matter how benign her presence, she might unwittingly agitate a bear. After half an hour without seeing anything but the beavers, we headed home.

When I returned to look for bears without the dog the next day, I wandered off the trail and sat on a log stump. A park ranger stood on the trail where I had earlier watched. He carried a shotgun and spoke intermittently on his hand-held radio. Hikers occasionally stopped to visit with him. When he wasn't talking on the radio or to passersby, he seemed restless, perhaps nervous. The sound of his boots scuffed on gravel. He checked the squelch on his radio. Checked his gun. It occurred to me that he didn't really want to see a bear.

As I sat and waited, I thought about the guys and their upcoming trip. I had no qualms about hunting as long as the animal was an abundant resource in the ecosystem and was treated respectfully both before and after its death. I could understand my husband's and sons' call to the outdoors during the riotous autumn of the year. And I appreciated the value of wild organic meat. Yet I knew there was something more to the killing; something primal and raw and incomprehensible that drew my husband and sons to the hunt. While the gun I once carried had been a means of protecting my children, it became something altogether different in their hands. Something entirely mysterious to me.

Eventually I got up from my log seat and went to talk to the ranger. I was curious to know when the last sighting had been and whether there had been trouble.

"No trouble," he said. "Not yet, anyway. Backpackers have been seeing him every few days and we're worried he's getting too used to people."

I asked him about the shotgun and what he intended to do if he saw the bear. He explained that he had several types of rounds for the shotgun. The goal was to teach the bear to avoid humans. The first shot would be a "cracker" round, a shell that transmitted a flash of light with a loud, crackling noise. The second choice was rubber bullets, a painful but not lethal reminder that people meant big trouble. Finally, the ranger had shells loaded with slugs, just in case a confrontation turned ugly and he needed to kill the bear.

I asked if he had ever killed a bear, and he said no—but that he'd had some close calls he didn't much care to think about. That evening the bear stayed away.

Alaska is home to three species of bears. Polar bears reside north of the Arctic Circle. Black bears come in a variety of colors ranging from light gray (glacier bear) to cinnamon brown and black. Brown and grizzly bears are names for a single species of bear. Home to ninety-eight percent of the United States' population of brown bears, Alaska is one of the few places in the world where brown bears can be hunted. The concentration of browns in central Alaska is one bear per fifteen-to-twenty-three square miles. On Kodiak Island the concentration is nearly one brown bear per square mile. The island's abundance of salmon also gives Kodiak bears the opportunity to gorge and grow inordinately large. It is here that many hunters seek out big game trophies.

Jim, the husband of a friend, told me about his bear experience on Kodiak Island. He had gone hunting with friends, and on the last day of the hunt he spotted a brown bear on the hillside several ridges away. It was getting late in the day, almost too late to shoot a bear. It would take hours to skin and pack out. Besides, he and his friends needed to reach their boat before dark and it was anchored several miles away in a secluded cove.

Jim remembered looking at the bear again and deciding it was just too good an opportunity to pass up. The hunt was nearly over and they still didn't have their trophy. This might be his only chance.

It took Jim longer to stalk the bear than he anticipated. His first shot wounded the animal and it stumbled into a stand of alders below the tree line. Jim hesitated. It would be foolish to follow a wounded bear into the brush. He also knew that, after hearing the rifle shot, the other hunters would be on their way. So he mentally marked the place where the bear had disappeared and went to meet them.

By this time Jim had hiked many miles over steep terrain and hadn't eaten since breakfast. The exertion and adrenaline of the hunt had depleted his last reserves of energy. Shortly after he met up with the other hunters, and as they returned to find the bear, Jim suddenly collapsed.

"I fell flat on my face. It was like a marathon runner that hits the wall'," Jim explained. The hunters stopped and let Jim rest and drink. They offered the last candy bar from someone's pocket. As the evening shadows began to lengthen, they resumed their hike and found the bear. It was dead, lying not far from where Jim had shot it.

The trek back to the water's edge became a struggle as they slogged through a knee-deep stream under the weight of the bear's hide. Adding to the tremendous exertion of the day, the chill of evening air and icy water seeped into Jim's bones. Every step became an act of sheer will; his movement seemed mechanical and forced as his limbs grew heavy with fatigue. He found himself beginning to stumble, a sign that he was growing hypothermic.

When they reached the cove, Jim suggested they leave him behind. The other hunters could move more quickly without him. Once they got to the boat, they could motor over and pick him up. He would build a fire as a marker along the dark shoreline.

The others agreed. It wasn't that much farther; the boat would be just a few miles down the beach. Within a couple of hours they'd be back. They left and Jim began collecting wood for the fire. It had rained earlier in the day, and the only dry wood was what he could find by crawling under the branches of broad spruce trees. He finally had enough kindling and dry grass to start a fire, and it was a good thing. He needed to get warm from the outside; his own body wasn't generating much heat.

With cold, trembling fingers he reached for the lighter. But his pocket was empty. Quickly he tried the other pockets. The lighter was gone. Either it had fallen out as he bent over to skin the bear or it had dropped out as he scrounged for wood. He tried to retrace his hunt for wood, but found himself shivering and growing disoriented in the dark. Rain began to drizzle.

He realized with sudden certainty that he was now in a

survival situation. He had no fire or food. All he had was a blood-soaked bear hide.

A bear hide.

The very bear whose life he had claimed, the bear that had culminated a great hunt, would now be the bear that would save his life. He unfolded the hide and rolled himself in it. Whatever part of Jim's clothing was not already wet, now became saturated in bear blood. But the hide was warm, warm enough to keep his teeth from chattering. Fitfully Jim slept in his womblike bed, dreaming bear dreams as he listened for the sound of a boat motor. He would not hear it until dawn of the next morning.

The third time I looked for the bear I went later in the evening. I positioned myself on the other side of the pond about 100 yards from the where the salmon, weak from their upstream migration to spawn in these waters, splashed below the crosshatch of wood that formed the dam. I sat behind a fan of exposed roots from a fallen tree. This time it didn't occur to me to look for an escape route.

I cannot explain my lack of fear. With each visit to this place, every nerve ending seemed to grow more aware of my surroundings. Even my uneasy thoughts about the upcoming hunt faded with the gentle echoes of evening light. I noticed the veins and capillaries of individual leaves on crimson cranberry bushes. The quiet stillness amplified the trickle of water over the dam. The smell of the air changed from the scent of grass to the tang of ripening berries and then to the cool musk of dirt and shadows. For over an hour I sat and watched. Eventually, even the whisper of bird wings grew quiet, and cool mist began to rise off the pond.

Then, like a ghost, he appeared. On the other the side of the dam, the brown bear ambled into the middle of the stream and sat down in the water facing me. I don't think he saw me, but if he did he was unconcerned. He dunked his head and then looked up. Water trickled off his ears and snout. He was sunny brown, an adolescent bear, maybe two years old, around 400 pounds. Still sitting, he lifted his front paws out of the water and then, comically, he allowed himself to fall over backwards. He rolled over, got back on all fours and then sat down again and watched the salmon. He didn't appear hungry or intent on anything in particular. He was lean and lanky, gorgeous and just a little bit goofy looking. Then as quickly as he appeared, he wandered off, his motions fluid and effortless and quiet.

Had I not been anchored by the weight of my own body, I might have flown with euphoria, lifted up and out of my skin into the cool evening sky by consuming joy. How wonderful to see this bear, undisturbed, playing almost humanlike with relaxed abandon. I stayed another hour, hoping he might return. Twice more I saw him cross the stream, each time a little farther away. Seeing the bear again proved he was real and not some wisp of wishful thinking. Then somehow I knew the bear was gone for good and it was time to go home.

At the dark end of dusk, the crunch of my footsteps on the trail made real my own presence here—a place as tangible and mysterious as the spaces of family and motherhood and the conflicted human world in which I lived. Yet for this moment, the taste of crisp night air eclipsed all else except the rising moon to the north.

MOUNT MARATHON

This summer, the season before Mark leaves for college, I've lost track of the miles. I only know I've grown stronger. Faster. In training for this race, I am learning about the body's resiliency. Its capacity to adapt. I am no athlete. If someone had told me, even five years ago, that I would someday run an uphill six-mile training run without stopping, I would have laughed. And yet, here I am getting ready to run the mountain race that Mark ran two years ago. The race I thought would kill him.

The Fourth of July Mount Marathon race began in 1909 as a bar room bet in Seward, Alaska. The coastal town sits at the edge of Resurrection Bay with mountains gathered like matriarchs around its crystalline waters. Old-time Sourdoughs bet whether it was possible for anyone to run to the top of the mountain and back in under one hour. The loser would buy drinks for the crowd. Local merchants got involved and upped the ante by contributing a suit of clothing and other wares. Thus began an Independence Day tradition that now attracts a multitude of people. Seward's population of 3,000 swells to 10,000 over the Fourth of July as spectators line the streets to watch runners begin and finish the trek. Race results are splashed across the front pages of newspapers statewide. The race is divided into three groups: men, women, and juniors under age seventeen.

Mark and Erik drove to Seward to watch the race when they were fifteen and seventeen years old. They could see the mountain trail from the streets of Seward, a steep climb of 3,022 feet. They joined the enthusiastic crowd as dirty, often bloodied runners came down from the mountain and pushed to the finish line. First under the wire was Brad Precosky, winning the race for a second consecutive year.

Mark returned from the race with shining eyes. Erik too was inspired, but he had long since relinquished competitive endeavors to his brother. Only when Mark entered high school and joined the cross-country ski team did Erik's sleepy competitive spirit awaken. Coaches marveled at how fast Erik, who had tootled along on the team for two years, suddenly began to ski. But that was the extent of Erik's athletic career, a brief burst of enthusiasm in an attempt to defeat his brother. In the end he preferred to cheer Mark on.

"I'm going to run Mount Marathon next year," Mark said, his jaw set in determination. "And I'm going to win."

I encouraged him, but hinted that participation itself was an accomplishment. Especially the first time. Mark ignored me and began training in earnest before the year was over. By spring he ate only foods that fed his growing muscles. He gulped vitamins, read about sports nutrition, and studied how to train for optimal performance. He regularly ran Arctic Valley Road, a six-mile uphill slog to the base of Rendezvous Peak. From there he hiked the trail to the top. On one of his training runs, he met defending champion Brad Precosky. Brad slowed his van and offered Mark a lift back down the mountain; running downhill is tough on the knees. Meeting the race's star runner only fueled Mark's motivation. As Brad dropped him off at the bottom of the hill, Mark said, "You and me, Brad. Number One."

Mark's confidence flabbergasted me. How could he make such claims? Wasn't he setting himself up for disappointment? He was running as a rookie. After all the big talk, wouldn't he be embarrassed if he didn't win?

Mark's good friend Daniel decided to run the race as well. The boys trained together. And they trained separately, secretly trying to gain a competitive edge on the other. I worried that their fierce competition might ruin a long-standing friendship.

"What happens if one of you falls on the mountain?" I asked. "Would you stop to help Daniel?"

Mark thought about this. "Only if no one else is around to help."

I was appalled.

The night before the race, all junior racers were required to attend a pre-race safety meeting with their parents in Seward. Before the meeting, we walked from our hotel to the base of the mountain. Sheer cliffs marked the final descent, a 200-foot nearly vertical wall of rock and loose shale.

"You're going up and down *that?*" I asked.

"Yup," Mark grinned. He and Daniel had already trained on these rocks, looking for the best way to negotiate the cliff. Although I'd read about the race in the newspaper, watched a bit of it on the evening news, and seen the trail from the streets of Seward, I had not begun to conceive the danger of this quest.

My fears were confirmed at the safety meeting later that evening. The cliffs were always a risk, but this year the real danger lay in the crevasse near the bottom of the snowfield. Many runners used the snow as a chute to quickly descend the upper portion of the mountain. Just days before, a runner, hurtling down the snow in an uncontrolled attempt to avoid the crevasse, had catapulted onto rocks and crushed his spine.

The crowd grew quiet as race official, Fred Moore, told the story.

"The last we've heard is that the guy will survive," Moore said. "But the last time he felt his legs was when he made the decision to take the snow chute. He'll never walk again."

Moore went on, "I was one of the people who stayed with him until a helicopter airlifted him off the mountain, and I can tell you this. No mountain and no race are worth what happened to him. Be careful out there."

I looked at Todd and at Daniel's father. Were they having the same trouble breathing that I was? Had we really agreed to allow our children to compete in this event? The whole race should be abolished, I thought. The mere idea of running the mountain began to seem like an egregious insult to common sense. The hammer of my heartbeat roared in my ears.

Back in our room I couldn't sit still. I felt as if my skin had been peeled away to expose every nerve ending. Erik was due into town any minute and I looked forward to his calming presence. He planned to drive to Seward after work that evening and meet us at the hotel. Todd watched the news and I wanted to cover my ears. It was all bad news. Terrible news. Then a local broadcaster announced a fatal accident involving a teenager on the Seward Highway, the one we had just traveled, the one Erik was driving as we watched television. *Name withheld pending notification of next of kin.*

I called home, no answer. Fleeing the throbbing light of the television, I walked the streets of Seward. Up and down each street and back and forth across each cross street, I walked. *Jesus*, I whispered over and over like a mantra, a call for help, a plea. A cool breeze blew off the ocean as the northern sun dipped below the Kenai Mountains. Sea gulls cried, circled the docks, and dove for remnants of the day's catch. Daylight even at 11 p.m., I walked until my bones ached. And I imagined losing two sons in a twenty-four-hour period. All because of a damned race.

The story unfolded before my eyes. Erik killed in the car accident as he comes to watch his brother's race. Mark, grief-stricken, runs the race anyway, runs it determined to win it for the sake of his brother. Mark launches himself down the cliffs and lands in a crumpled heap at the bottom. And like that awful wait at Devil's Pass, I imagine their funerals. The terrible abyss of their absence.

I found myself at the cliffs, peering up at what lay ahead. Shadows deepened among spruce trees as the night settled into the long twilight before a 3 a.m. sunrise. Here my prayers grew more articulate. Less frantic. I cannot claim that prayers brought real peace; only resignation and the flicker of hope that God would take charge of what I had no control over. But this much was absolutely sure to me: I knew without question that Mark would either win tomorrow's race or come off the mountain on a stretcher.

I returned to the room after midnight and called home again. Erik answered and something inside my chest broke free and flew. "They shut down the road after the accident. I had to turn around and go home," he explained. "I'll be there tomorrow morning."

"Please be careful," I said, my voice as wavering and unsteady as my legs.

The morning dawned cool and cloudy, perfect running weather. The junior's competition was first up at 9:15 a.m. Mark hardly looked at us as he prepared for the race. His mouth was set in a grim line. Volunteers at the first-aid station taped his ankles and then he wrapped duct tape around the top edge of his running shoes to keep out the mountain's loose scree and gravel. As the crowd began to gather along the sidewalks of Seward, Mark stretched and jogged to warm up. Daniel arrived smiling and chatting with his father. How relaxed he seemed. Why did Mark seem so angry? Or was he just intent? After all these years, I still could not read him.

An ambulance waited at the bottom of the cliffs. A stretcher lay perched halfway up the incline. This, I was told, was routine race procedure.

I decided to watch from the starting line.

The gun fired and Mark and Daniel led the pack along the streets toward the mountain. The crowd cheered the six-block route to the cliffs. I paced and listened to the announcer's commentary.

Vendors had set up their wares along the side streets and a nauseating soup of smells wafted from the popping Kettle corn and cooking hot dogs. Mark and Daniel's friends and their families had begun to arrive and everyone I met seemed to know the boys' ambitions. I could only nod at their encouragement and good wishes for our sons. I waited and looked at my watch.

"We have the first junior runners making it to the turnaround point," the announcer said over the loudspeaker. "Coming first around the turn is bib number one-seventy-seven, Mark Johnson, with bib number one-sixty-seven, Daniel Andrews, in close pursuit."

I grabbed the arm of someone next to me and said, "That's them! They're first and second!" The woman grinned with enthusiasm. I squinted up at the mountain and saw only the dots of runners as they wound up the steep trail. The boys still had to get down the cliffs in one piece. I wished I had binoculars. I paced and picked my way through the throng of people. An acquaintance stopped to talk, then another, and I smiled as I tried to listen both to their conversations and any news over the loudspeaker. Suddenly I heard the crowd begin to stir.

"Ladies and gentlemen!" the announcer cried. "The first runners are on their way to the finish line and today we may have the closest first-place finish in race history!"

There came Mark and Daniel, stride for stride around the corner of Fourth Avenue. Dirty and slick with sweat, as they approached the last 100 yards, Daniel pulled several strides ahead. Mark's face contorted with fury. He lengthened his stride and pumped his arms. The roar of the crowd deafened my own screams as I began pushing through people toward the finish line. Just seconds under the wire, Mark pulled ahead, finishing the race just two strides and one second ahead of his buddy.

The boys collapsed on the other side of the finish line. Camera crews descended upon them. At first they could not speak. Their chests heaved as their lungs gasped for air. Eventually they helped each other up, high-fived, and then draped their arms around each other's shoulders as news teams stormed them with questions. Someone handed them water. I snapped pictures and told anyone who would listen. "They did it! They're best friends and they did it together!"

All nightmares of the previous evening evaporated in the rush of excitement. Todd and Erik came to the finish line after watching the boys descend the cliffs, wondering who had won. Daniel's parents too, wondered what had happened. As I described it to them, their eyes moistened with tears. Most glorious of all, blessing beyond all blessings, the boys had finished the race with their bodies and friendship intact.

We placed Mark's trophy on the sofa table in our living room among the collection of family photos and snapshots of the boys. Every time I looked at it I marveled at my son, at his colossal determination. Over the next weeks, Mark's eyes glistened with pride as people congratulated him on his victory. He was gratified at Daniel's close second and talked about his win in the plural "we."

Mark was also nonchalant, shrugging and grinning as friends slapped him on the back. "No one else even came close," he said. "They couldn't touch us."

I could not begrudge his swagger. He'd earned it. Besides, when it came down to the things that mattered most, I had gained confidence that he would do the right thing. Earlier in the summer he'd forfeited a top position in a training race to help a mountain biker who had fallen and dislocated her elbow.

I remembered how I had pressed Mark to climb Mount Baldy all those years ago, insisting that he share my ambition for the top. I thought of how I'd overestimated his ability then—and how I'd underestimated him on this race. I always managed to misjudge him. Ruefully I wondered if I'd ever get it right.

The summer of Mark's departure, I knew I needed a goal, something to keep my mind and body occupied the months before he went off to college. Running Mount Marathon seemed like a fitting tribute to Mark, an acknowledgment of his achievement and a last ditch effort to connect with my youngest child before he left home. If I was the one who pushed him up Mount Baldy, he was the one who now inspired my run up Mount Marathon. Maybe by running the race, I would learn what I still did not understand about him. And maybe I would gain some measure of respect from a young man whose irreverence passed as a wickedly funny sense of humor.

But as my stride grew stronger over the months of training, something changed. The race grew into more than a tribute, more than a farewell, although it was all these things. Some awakening desire drove me forward.

I ran now because I could. I ran because, like backpacking in high country, pushing myself beyond discomfort told me something about myself. Slowly my body acquiesced to my will. When I lay in bed, I could see muscle definition in my thighs and calves; these legs hardly seemed to belong to me. Remember, I am no athlete. But I was growing strong. Someone told me a month before the race that I looked "scrappy." I laughed and considered it a compliment of the highest order. I ran because filling my lungs with the smell of rain on raspberry bushes hinted at the scent of heaven.

And then there was the mountain. It was tough. The first time I climbed it I thought my lungs would burst inside my chest. I climbed the steepest sections on all-fours, like Spiderwoman. I darkened the gray scree with sweat and spit and snot. Topping the jagged ridge, I wondered where along the way I should turn around. Being in the clouds, I could not see the trail back down the mountain. So I continued until the path became a narrow game trail. Then in a swirl of fog an enormous mountain goat, a billy, appeared. Seeing him before he saw me, and only ten yards away, I crouched down just as he turned his black eyes to peer curiously at me. Great swatches of the previous winter's white fur dangled off his body. He had shiny, spiked black horns, a square body and face, and black, two-toed hooves adept at scrambling the flinty slopes. I wondered how he managed in this terrain of rocks and cliffs and sky. He appeared so confident, at ease, even in the improbable presence of a human.

We gazed at each other for some time before he ambled down the steep side of the ledge and out of view.

By this time my legs had begun to cramp and the mountain breeze had cooled my sweat enough to create a chill. I continued a bit farther, but as the trail gave way to snow with no footprints except that of the goat, I quickly realized I had missed my turn-around point. On the sliding run down, the clouds parted and the city of Seward emerged at the foot of the mountain. The waters of Resurrection Bay glittered in the sunshine. Fishing boats, like toys, bobbed in the bay. At the midway point, rocks gave way to a steep meadow abloom in wildflowers. Wild geranium, columbine, and forget-me-nots splashed their colors along the hillside. The trail followed a creek bed that fed into the area of the cliffs—the area where an ambulance and stretcher await on race day. Here the mountain became a puzzle, a jigsaw of trails and rock faces and roots. Which way, then, to the bottom?

Since that run the mountain owned me. I lay in bed at night, wondering the best way up and down. I read running magazines. Like Mark did two years before, I took vitamins and wondered how to optimize my performance during the race. I alternated long runs with shorter, more intense workouts. Todd teased that I was acting as though I wanted to win it—as laughable an idea to me as it was to him.

By fate or by choice, no one in my family would be here to watch the race. Todd was out of town. The boys were traveling together in Europe, their first summer away from family and Alaska. Running without their presence in the crowd seemed entirely appropriate somehow. My sons had undertaken a healthy quest to find themselves; their task was not to hold my hand through a journey that was ultimately my own.

But secretly, I harbored the fantasy that they would all be there to surprise me at the finish line. Like the longing for a picture of myself in a son's scrapbook. Even in the best relationships, we manage to disapoint each other.

Arctic Valley Road is a gravel trek that winds six miles uphill toward the trail to Rendezvous Peak, the mountain I climbed from the other side two summers ago, the season Erik left for college. I watch for bears, but so far I've seen only ground squirrels, ptarmigan, and spruce hens. The second third of this run is steepest. It takes all my concentration to put one foot in front of the other. I calculate fractions and times and distances, inventing elaborate computations that indicate how far I've come and how far I have yet to go. When the going gets particularly tough, I pretend that individual spruce trees along the road rally for me. "You can do it," the tall one on the corner of the upcoming curve says in its silent way. "You're looking strong." Passing that tree I see another tall spruce in a thicket of alder beckoning. "You're almost there," this one says. "The toughest part is nearly over." And when early in my training I had to stop and walk, the trees forgave me, encouraged me, and exuded confidence that next time I'd make it a little farther. Along with the alder and dust, along with the fragrance of green grass and sunshine, I breathed in the scent of myself as sweat trickled down my neck.

As the run has grown easier, I've taken to daydreaming. The fullness of summer has changed my view. In early spring, when bare alders and birch branches rattled in the wind I could see the entire basin below through their barren limbs. Lengthening days and warmer sunshine produce abundant foliage that now fills the overlook of the valley. From this vantage I can only lift my eyes to the hills and keep running.

I run mountains because I cannot run after sons who are leaving me. I run looking for a trail that at the moment seems hidden in the mist. Somewhere along the way I hope I will find my confidence and ease among the uncertain terrain of the future.

An unexpected breeze caresses my hot skin as I push through the final stretch of road. To the pounding of footsteps, to the rhythm of a beating heart, my spirit sings, "*Thank you . . . thank you . . . thank you.*"

WILD BOYS: AN EPILOGUE

You were my dream.

I am running, breathing hard, my mind growing clear the way it does after the heart pumps clutter from the brain and the words come.

You were my dream.

My step quickens as I run, as though the words have somehow infused me with strength. A stiff wind dances in the trees, a sure sign of yet another changing season. Summer has grown gilded around the edges. Hints of color—a splash of yellow here, a dash of red there—flirt with the mountain's foliage. As I run, I remember.

The boys were babies, both in diapers, and I walked in a haze of exhaustion and low-grade malaise. I could not think clearly, my mind seemed wrapped in gauze of weary emotion. I was lonely. Drained. My babies' cries felt like the foreshadowing of imminent disaster which only I, as their mother, could avert. Yet I yearned for a reprieve, a respite, if only for a few hours. The few blessed moments of sleep between night nursings hardly seemed enough to keep me functioning and I found my confidence crumbling when even the most basic task grew perplexing. I once made grape juice and later could not find the pitcher I'd made it in. I scoured the refrigerator, the cupboards, the closets, and finally discovered the pitcher in the cabinet with the laundry soap. I wondered about my sanity, my fitness to care for my precious sons, who along with wearing me out, delighted me beyond imagination.

Only my mother seemed to understand but she was 2,000 miles away and our budget could not accommodate the length or number of long-distance phone calls that I craved.

When I beseeched my husband for a remedy, I could hardly articulate the problem much less formulate a solution. I could not describe to him my sense of drowning without it sounding like I did not love my family. Just the opposite was true—I was consumed by this new role as mother. We tried a few dates just the two of us, trading babysitting with another mom in the neighborhood. But Todd seemed distracted and self-conscious—as though he was no longer sure he knew me. We were on different wavelengths altogether.

One day I dissolved into tears, begging my husband for some sort of consolation. Surely someday my life would find normalcy, I would return to myself, I would dream again. Right?

Todd, whose formidable workload was made more difficult by interrupted sleep, and who was surely feeling the pressure of his own increasing family responsibilities, lost his patience with me.

"Grown-ups don't dream silly dreams," he snapped. "You're a mother. It's time to grow up."

We stood in the kitchen of the Arkansas military housing. I held Mark in my arms, his sleeping form melding into my own. Erik, wearing nothing but a diaper, sat on the cool floor stirring clothespins in a pot.

"Since when did 'growing up' mean giving up your dreams?" I cried. Rather than a rope to pull me ashore, Todd had tossed me a stone and as I wrapped myself around his words I felt myself sinking, sinking, into dark waters from which I would not soon emerge. Drifting downward my lungs burned, my heart pounded, my head nearly burst from the pressure of packing embryonic dreams into some tightly sealed corner of myself. At the age of twenty-two, how could I surrender youth when I had just so recently become aware of its power? And while Todd had spoken out of his own frustration, I believed that holding on to that stone would keep me from being swept into a wild current that might deny my commitments, my obligations, even the vows of marriage.

Only the passing years could teach me that dreams are not as dangerous as they might seem.

When Erik was six years old, I wrote him a letter that I knew I would not give him for many years.

> *January 1990*
>
> *Here you are, Erik, nearing the end of your first-grade year with a loose tooth, a thirst for knowledge, and an unshakable confidence in the future. Watching you grow has filled me with joy that I never dreamed possible seven years ago when you lay kicking around inside me.*
>
> *Now you face the world nearly bursting with ideas and ideals. You simmer with plans for weather machines and mouse traps. You build wonderful snowmobiles with scrap lumber, a few nails, and a paper towel (for a sail maybe?). You solve mysteries of the missing bird bones that you stacked carefully on the porch and that disappeared overnight. You build rockets with twine as a wick to its candle engines.*

Hold fast to those dreams, Erik. They are the key to youth; the key to change in the world. All of your life people will tell you why your ideas won't work, without offering an alternative that will. Even now, however unwittingly, people dismiss a weather machine as silly; smile at an empty mouse trap; and offer stray dogs as an explanation for missing bones. Learn along the way, son, but never let knowledge discourage you.

Don't stop at what others say can't be done. Most likely it is something they simply would not choose to do themselves, something they lack the vision for. Don't let others define realistic expectations. "Realistic" is often a term for mediocrity. Your own definition will prove far more inspiring, and the nails you pound through your own hard work will build a life you can be proud to acknowledge.

Finally, if growing up means surrendering your dreams then choose to stay young. Without dreams there is no hope. Without hope, what future is in store for the world? Without hope youth fades and shrivels like a thirsty flower. Stay young, Erik, no matter what your age. Mom

I tucked the letter away in his baby book. I gave it to him the summer I climbed Rendezvous Peak, the summer he graduated from high school. The summer that began the season of our leaving.

You were my dream.

I dreamed of animals. I used the boys as an excuse to get a puppy, a kitten, and rabbits. They never asked for these pets until my suggestion put the happy idea in their minds. I rationalized that caring for pets would develop a sense of responsibility and help teach the boys how to care for something outside themselves. All of this was true. But what was also true is that these creatures mopped up the overflow of my need to nurture; they returned my attention with uncomplicated affection. I loved their company and how they became a part of our family.

My heart pirouetted as little boys lavished hugs on a dog who returned their adoration with a pink tongue and a tail that wagged hard enough to knock them over. I laughed when the kitten leaped from bed to bed and trounced on the boys' toes as they drifted off to sleep. As I ushered the unruly little tabby into the garage, I smiled at Mark's palpable indignation at feline rudeness.

The rabbits in their outdoor hutches slept in straw beds and in winter the ice had to be broken on their water dishes. They were the closest we could come, on our quarter-acre lot, to caring for livestock. Erik liked the way bunny noses twitched and how their whiskers tickled his cheek when he held them. And when Mark decided he *must* have a rat for a pet, I reluctantly agreed. The naked-tailed rodent earned, if not my affection, at least my admiration for her surprising intelligence and her tender hold on my son. Mark played hide and seek with the rat under his blankets, fed it Fruit Loops, and laughed when she used her prehensile-like paws to grasp his nose and look inside a nostril. One day I peeked into the opened crack of Mark's bedroom and witnessed a solemn and private ceremony.

In one hand, Mark held his beloved rat. In the other he held a tiny sea shell full to the brim with water. He promptly poured the water on the unsuspecting creature's head. Making the sign of the cross, Mark said "I baptize you in the name of the Father and the Son and the Holy Spirit."

He then held the damp bewildered animal up and spoke kindly to her face. "Now," he said, "we'll both go to heaven."

Our dog was also an excuse for me to leave the house every few evenings for a walk. I did not have the fortitude to say "I need to get out," nor could I explain my meaning of the word "need." Instead I said, "The dog must get some exercise," which was true. I walked under the starlit sky and breathed the cold air and listened to my boots crunch on snow, while the dog's collar jangled in the dark. I thought about my sons and about our family and sometimes wondered what would become of us. I was often inexplicably sad.

I dreamed of being a writer. When we finally had a few dollars to spare and a reliable neighbor who would trade babysitting duties for a few hours at a time, I returned to school to become a teacher. In our discussion of the future, Todd challenged me: If I could, in the four years it would take to complete a teaching degree, guarantee teacher's pay in some field of writing, then I should write. Otherwise, teacher's pay and benefits with summers off would be ideal for the family. Since I could not guarantee a stable, lucrative writing career, and since I truly liked children, I chose teaching. I enjoyed my classes, soaked in knowledge like a thirsty sponge, and regained some confidence in my mental capabilities. Then, attempting to forge a better family life with less time away from home, Todd left the Air Force and again I quit school, this time to work. Employed at a number of jobs (some of them simultaneously), and always gravitating toward publishing and writing, I found myself the editor (an editor!) of a small monthly newspaper. In four years—the time it would have taken to finish school—I was making the equivalent of first-year teacher's pay. Does life not take some splendid turns?

And I dreamed of a life in the wilderness. How richly Alaska colored in the sketch of that dream! And how grand it was to share it with two growing boys. Our small rectangular, cedar-sided house even looked like a cabin, tucked as it was among the spruce and birch trees of First Street. Inside, the rock fireplace was made from angular gray stones found near a fishing village called Hope. We lived within walking distance of a mountain ridge, and together the boys and I explored the wooded trails that led to it. When they were old enough (just barely) Erik and Mark rode their bikes to the woods where they built forts and climbed trees and learned that devil's club stings and that high-bush cranberries grow sweeter after the first frost. We grew in tune with the undulating rhythms of the land, became familiar with individual trees on the hillside whose colors signaled the changing seasons. Later, we learned our capacity for endurance as we trekked along mountain ridges. And we considered the shadowed mysteries of life and death as we harvested salmon and cut up the meat that would feed our family for the coming year.

My sons became wild boys, nurtured by the mountains and the rivers and the sky. They drew their sustenance from the wilderness, grew strong and healthy and confident in the cradle of her expansive arms. She took hold of them and gripped them with her power and fiercely taught them more than I ever could.

Since Erik moved into an apartment of his own—where a picture of me is tacked on the wall in his bedroom without my asking—he writes poetry and stories that affirm that these wild boys are on their way to becoming men of wisdom and grace.

You were my dream.

And now, curled deep below the blue waters of two decades, new dreams stir and stretch and press against the membrane of memory and sky.

About the Author

KAYLENE JOHNSON is a professional writer and longtime Alaskan and the author of the New York Times Bestseller, Sarah: How a Hockey Mom Turned Alaska's Political Establishment Upside Down. Her award-winning articles have appeared in Alaska magazine, the Los Angeles Times, Spirit magazine, and other publications. She holds a BA from Vermont College and an MFA in Writing from Spalding University in Louisville, Kentucky.

PRAISE FOR A TENDER DISTANCE

Family & Relationships. A TENDER DISTANCE: ADVENTURES RAISING MY SONS IN ALASKA by Kaylene Johnson (Alaska Northwest Books, 204 pages, softcover, $16.95, 978-0-88240-772-2): contributor to Alaska magazine and the Los Angeles Times presents parenting on a "high-voltage tightrope" between adventure and safety in rugged conditions; among the references are a torrent at Devil's Pass, a ghost bear on Kodiak Island, and mom's comment about Mark and Erik who were "nurtured by the mountains and the rivers and the sky," growing strong and healthy in the "cradle of their expansive arms."

—*Foreword Footnotes*

With a journalist's quick eye and a spiritual observer's shining soul, the remarkable Kaylene Johnson measures the growth of her two boys as they come of age in Alaska's wilderness in her new book, A Tender Distance. The intrepid Johnson confronts physical danger in all its forms from bears to avalanches, and then she lets gratitude in all its forms match those dangers. In these heart-in-your-mouth tales Johnson first tries to guide, and then realizes she must merely watch in anxious awe as her sons encounter their wilderness without and within. Johnson's fierce balancing makes these amazing adventures a mother's coming of age, too. The essays in Tender Distance challenge us to stand on our precipices, looking out on what it means to be truly alive.

—MOLLY PEACOCK, poet and creative nonfiction writer,
a former Poet-in-Residence at the American Poet's
Corner and one of the creators of Poetry in Motion on
buses and subways throughout North America

Like a brilliant fall day, Kaylene Johnson's A Tender Distance has a gorgeous ache of melancholy coursing through its pages. This lyrical book about raising children, set against the vast uncompromising landscape of a primeval country, shows us well that with every coming there must be a leaving, that from the moment they're born our children are ebbing from us. A Tender Distance is written with a calm, deep grace. It is a poem of a book, suffused with courage, sadness and beauty.

—Richard Goodman, author of *French Dirt:*
The Story of a Garden in the South of France and
The Soul of Creative Writing